OP 1st 15th

Lacking d. w.

THE BOBBY RICHARDSON STORY

The Bobby Richardson Story

Bobby Richardson

FLEMING H. REVELL COMPANY
Westwood, New Jersey

Preface

Every once in a while Bobby Richardson gets a letter from an irate and anonymous fan berating him for an error, or for failure to hit with three men on, and asking him, "What kind of a guy are you, anyway?" It's a good question, and there are several good answers.

To those who play with him on the New York Yankees, to the critics, and to those of us who just like to watch him from the grandstand, he looks good. One sportswriter says of him that "He doesn't smoke, drink, cuss or chew—and he doesn't take a back seat to any second baseman in baseball." Casey Stengel once said that at the beginning of a season he could just put Bobby out there and forget about second base for the rest of the year. Opposing batters try to hit away from him, but he has an arm like a rifle and a pair of lightning legs.

It wasn't always so; he got there the hard way, tasting disappointment and defeat, getting more "boo's" than cheers. (Once he tried to steal second with a teammate already *on* second!) He has known the frustration of being shipped off to minor league clubs in Richmond and Denver; he has been pulled out to "warm the bench" in many a game. All his life he has fought the handicap of being comparatively small, physically: he stood only 5 feet 8 inches and weighed a mere 150 pounds when he broke into big-time baseball, and he stands only 5 feet 9 inches and weighs 170 today. A Yankee scout who watched him play on an American Legion team in Charleston, S. C., thought he was a good aggressive infielder, but too little for major league ball.

But he had fire, spirit, "fight." In his knee-high-to-a-grasshopper days, he would cry on rainy days, because then he couldn't play ball. From dawn to dark, he played. He studied the big pros, and made up his mind that he wanted to play like Stan Musial of the St. Louis Cardinals. He was impressed when he saw the popular athletes around his native town of Sumter going to Sunday school or church on Sundays, with their Bibles under their arms.

It was in Sumter that he knew the two greatest days of his life, up to now. One was the day when he both graduated from high school and signed his first Yankee contract; the other (he calls it "the most important day") came when, at fourteen, he had a personal chat with God, during which "I saw, for the first time really, that a live, flesh-and-blood Person had suffered an agonizing death because of love for a boy named Robert Richardson. In that moment a tiny flame of desire was kindled in me, a desire to know this Man, to follow Him, to show my gratitude, and though there have been detours along the way, that flame has never gone out."

Now two flames burned within him; they fused into

one. There was the determination to excel at his job, to be the best on the keystone sack. He was "that kind of guy." He accepted the setbacks, the hitting slumps, the bobbled plays as his wife and No. 1 coach Betsy suggested that he accept them. Betsy reminded him that Romans 8:28 had a message for him in the words ". . . all things work together for good to them that love God . . ."—even errors, and striking out. He made two costly errors (he's human!) in the 1964 World Series, but he also chalked up a new record of 13 hits in a single Series, and hit safely in 7 games.

You can see the two flames burning together in his words explaining how the desire to be both good athlete and good Christian have merged to make him "the sort of guy" he is today: "I realize simply that it is God who has given me the ability, the opportunity and certainly any earthly glory that might come through playing ball. I enjoy the sport I am in, but only because I feel that this is where God would have me serve Him." The less religious among his admirers and fans may think he should give a little more credit to his own fighting determination to reach the top, but all of them will admit that however the credit is assigned, he has come through it to a *character* that only the consuming twin desires to be good athlete *and* good follower of Christ could produce. No hint of scandal appears on his record; no lowering of the Christian moral standard is evident. He has never permitted his name to be used in a liquor or cigarette advertisement. He does, however, occasionally

break one firm Yankee rule—the one that forbids players responding to calls from the sidelines or the stands;
when some well-meaning friend shouts "Hey, Bobby!"
from the stands, he just can't bring himself to ignore it
and perhaps hurt an old friend. And he'll stop to chat
—and pay the ten-dollar fine. That's typical.

Ralph Houk, the Yankee General Manager, calls him
the best second baseman he has ever known—and, which
is more important, in the character department, "the
type of person I think all fathers would like to see their
children grow up to be." We agree. We give you Bobby
Richardson, big leaguer on the diamond and in the
Kingdom, a champ on second base—and a Christian
gentleman.

THE PUBLISHERS

Contents

Contents

Robert Clinton Richardson

Signed by Yankee Organization on June 12, 1953.

Led the American League in times at bat (679) in 1964, for the third consecutive year, tying an American League record. Also holds the American League record for the most at bats in one season—692 in 1962.
Led the Yankees in hits (181) in 1964.
Led American League in times at bat (630) in 1963.
Led Yankees in times at bat (630), hits (167) and stolen bases (15) in 1963.

Placed second to Mantle in American League's MVP Poll of 1962.
Set American League record for most times at bat (692) in 1962.
Set World Series record for the most hits in a 7-game series—13 in 1964 vs. St. Louis.

One of ten players to hit grand-slam homer in World Series game, connecting in first inning off Clem Labine of Pittsburgh on Oct. 8, 1960 at Stadium.
Most runs batted in in one World Series game (6—Oct. 8, 1960) and most RBIs in a World Series (12—1960 vs. Pittsburgh).
Tied World Series record for most runs scored in a World Series (8) vs. Pittsburgh, 1960.
Tied World Series record by hitting 2 triples in one World Series game vs. Pittsburgh, Oct. 12, 1960.

Won SPORT Magazine Corvette as outstanding performer, 1960 World Series.
Tied World Series record for most hits in a five-game series. (9—1961 vs. Cincinnati).

Year	Club	G	AB	R	H	2B	3B	HR	RBI	BB	SO	BA
1953	Norfolk	27	76	6	16	1	0	0	5	10	5	.211
1953	Olean	32	131	36	54	14	0	1	14	18	2	.412
1954	Binghamton	141	552	81	171	29	9	3	55	60	22	.310
1955	Denver	119	494	99	146	21	12	6	59	48	29	.296
1955	New York	11	26	2	4	0	0	0	3	2	0	.154
1955	Richmond	25	93	11	26	4	2	0	8	8	4	.280
1956	New York	5	7	1	1	0	0	0	0	0	1	.143
1956	Denver	124	534	102	175	30	12	10	73	29	32	.328
1957	New York	97	305	36	78	11	1	0	19	9	26	.256
1958	New York	73	182	18	45	6	2	0	14	8	5	.247
1959	New York	134	469	53	141	18	6	2	33	26	20	.301
1960	New York	150	460	45	116	12	3	1	26	35	19	.252
1961	New York	162	662	80	173	17	5	3	49	30	23	.261
1962	New York	161	692	99	209	38	5	8	59	37	24	.302
1963	New York	151	630	72	167	20	6	3	48	25	22	.265
1964	New York	159	679	90	181	25	4	4	50	28	36	.267
M. L. Totals		1103	4112	496	1115	147	32	21	301	200	176	.271

WORLD SERIES RECORD

Year	Club	G	AB	R	H	2B	3B	HR	RBI	BB	SO	BA
1957	New York	2	0	0	0	0	0	0	0	0	0	.000
1958	New York	4	5	0	0	0	0	0	0	0	0	.000
1960	New York	7	30	8	11	2	2	1	12	1	1	.367
1961	New York	5	23	2	9	1	0	0	0	0	0	.391
1962	New York	7	27	3	4	0	0	0	0	3	1	.148
1963	New York	4	14	0	3	1	0	0	0	1	3	.214
1964	New York	7	32	3	13	2	0	0	3	0	2	.406
	W. S. Totals	36	131	16	40	6	2	1	15	5	7	.305

ALL-STAR GAME RECORD

Year	Club	G	AB	R	H	2B	3B	HR	RBI	BB	SO	BA
1962	American	2	1	1	0	0	0	0	0	0	0	.000
1963	American	1	2	0	0	0	0	0	0	0	0	.000
1964	American	1	4	0	1	0	0	0	0	0	1	.250
	A. S. Totals	4	7	1	1	0	0	0	0	0	1	.143

Information by permission of New York Yankees Inc.

1

The Big Question

FROM THE YANKEE dugout I watched a drizzling rain fall on a long, dismal doubleheader in Baltimore. It was August 19, 1955—I remember the day because it was my birthday. In honor of the occasion Betsy Dobson—later to become my wife—had traveled to see me from my home town, Sumter, South Carolina.

The crowd in the Baltimore stadium was sparse and from the dugout I could see Betsy, pretty as a bouquet, sitting wistfully alone in a section of the stands.

My thoughts were as bleak as the surroundings. For days I had been struggling with a problem that seemed insoluble. I watched a man approach Betsy and attempt to strike up a conversation. That went on for about an inning and a half until the stranger gave up.

Betsy didn't see much of me. I was sent in for an inning or two in the first game, then benched.

I'd been called up from the Yankees' Triple A Denver Club on August 5 and played in 11 games for the major leaguers. The dugout was my home most of the time, and when I did play my performance at the plate was terrible. I fouled out, struck out, grounded out, popped out—everything but hit. I recorded one single during those 11 games.

Adding to my discouragement was a newspaper article in which Casey Stengel, then manager of the Yanks, was said to have pegged me as another good-field-no-hit infielder. My .154 average during the 11 games seemed to prove his point.

I hadn't gone into baseball to try to be rich or famous. I'd become a Christian at fourteen and believed that my life's purpose was to please God. I had a lot to learn about the Lord, and still do, but I'd always felt that my interest in the sport had been given to me by God and I was in it to glorify Him.

But doubt was gnawing at me now. *Had God really called me into professional baseball?*

When the last game of the doubleheader finally concluded (I can't remember who won either game) I couldn't get to the clubhouse fast enough to change and meet Betsy. The team was moving out to Cleveland that night and I knew I'd have only a few hours with her before leaving.

Halfway through dressing, I saw a coach coming toward me. He said, "Stengel wants to see you in his office."

I went on lacing up my shoes, but I had some real qualms. What did Casey want with me at this hour of the night?

A few moments later I found out. The man who

probably knew baseball as well as any other man alive was busy packing his uniform and equipment into a duffel bag when I walked in.

"Bobby," he said in his gruff tone, "We're going to make a change. We need to bring up a pitcher and we have to make room on the roster. We're going to send you out to Charleston, West Virginia."

What a birthday present! I knew the club needed pitching help, and until September 1 league rules permitted each club to carry no more than 25 players. Somebody had to go, and a spare infielder boasting a .154 average was a pretty good choice. But Charleston!

"That club's in the same league I just came from—only they're in last place," I told him.

"Yeah, I know," he drawled, stuffing several pairs of socks into the bag. "But I figure, if they're in last place, they won't be in any playoffs and you'll be able to come back up and join us in September."

Case was telling me to see the traveling secretary for meal money, tickets, and such but all I could think was, *"Lord, what's going on? I'm in baseball for You but I'm being sent back. I didn't make it!"*

A few minutes later, when I saw Bill McCory, the traveling secretary, I found out I was going to Richmond of the International League, not Charleston of the American Association. Richmond was also last in its league but it didn't change my feelings—except to wonder if Casey was wrong too about calling me back in September.

McCory told me Richmond was on the road at the

time and I'd have to join the team in Columbus, Ohio. First I'd have to go back to New York to pick up the rest of my gear.

I had a frantic chase to the bus outside the stadium where, just in time, I saved my suitcase from being shipped off to Cleveland.

By the time everything was straightened out and I had my suitcase in hand, the stands were closed. Betsy had waited as long as she could, then had retired to the lobby where I found her alone, patiently waiting.

I didn't have the heart to tell her the news then, so I hailed a cab and listened in silence all the way back to the hotel as she gaily chatted about the doubleheader. She tried to sound encouraging about the trifling part I had played but it only added to my misery.

The truth had to be told, however, and when we left the cab I tried to get it out quickly and easily, as though it were all part of the routine. But she knew me well enough even then to sense I was unhappy.

"You mean they're sending you back—right after calling you up?"

I tried to explain about the roster and how I'd be returning in September. But I knew a lot of factors were involved and coming back wasn't quite as automatic as Casey in his kindness had made it sound. A hundred thousand things could happen. What if I hit a slump at Richmond? What if another minor league infielder got hot, so hot he couldn't be ignored?

The Big Question

Baseball is a sport, but big league baseball is a serious business. And I knew the men who ran the business had to be convinced they were getting the best return from their investment.

Betsy brought me back to reality. "The Lord knows what He's doing, Robert. Don't let Satan get you discouraged. We ought to count our blessings. Look how good the Lord has been to you!" But there were big tears in her eyes, and inside I felt the same way.

At the hotel we went up to her room and passed the news on to her mother. Mrs. Dobson listened sympathetically. She knew what it meant but she was philosophical about it. "Well, you let us know where you wind up and what your schedule is."

I took a late train for New York that night, knowing Betsy and her mother would be on their way south again early the next morning.

It had been hard to say goodbye to Betsy, harder than I'd thought it would be, and homesickness was a dull ache inside when I thought of Sumter. The girl I loved was going back to the quiet, tree-shaded loveliness of the town where I'd grown up. But where was *I* going?

I leaned my forehead against the train window and watched the street lights of a nameless town hurtle by. I tried to push the question away but it kept coming back.

"Lord, do You really want me in baseball?"

2
Early Years

MY FATHER NEVER had any doubt about my place in the will of God. "Someday he'll be in the major leagues!"—that was his statement the day I was born. And he reminded my mother of his prediction seventeen years later on the day I signed with the Yankees.

Dad's interest in the game went back years before I entered the picture. He had played shortstop on the local sandlots and occasionally pitched. From men who knew him and played with him I gathered that he was a deft fielder and dependable at bat.

This kind of information could never have been drawn from my father. He was a quiet, unassuming man who dedicated his life to hard work. The time left over he gave to his family, to baseball, and to hunting—in that order.

We didn't talk much about his dream for my future. It was just understood as a fact and I accepted it long before I could tell one major league team from another.

I don't know exactly when I stopped living in my

father's enthusiasm and began to feel an attraction to the game myself. But as early as I can remember, I had a ball in my hands, throwing or trying to catch it. Baseballs, ping pong balls, tennis balls, basketballs—anything that could be lobbed against a wall and rebounded or tossed to somebody else who'd toss it back.

I used to give my mother gray hair by tossing an orange to her from across the kitchen—without warning. She lectured and fussed but without much conviction. She knew Dad and I had an unspoken agreement—I was to be a baseball player, come what may.

My sister Inez, one year older, didn't share my interest in sports. A quiet, studious girl, her interests were more typically feminine—dolls, playing house, writing letters.

My younger sister Willie Ann was exactly the opposite. Like me, she was noisy, always in a hurry, and for years could peg a ball across the backyard as well as I could. Although we played catch occasionally, we went our separate ways, too competitive to play together for long.

The rear of the two-story frame house we lived in was braced by a big chimney. It was perfect for throwing against, and I'd practice by the hour, firing a tennis ball at it and trying to scoop up the grounder that came bounding back. Unfortunately our house was old and its interior walls were plastered. Almost every time I missed the chimney and sent the ball thudding against the siding, a chunk of plaster fell off a wall inside. That was sure to bring my mother to the back door with a frown of disapproval.

"Mama, I was throwing at the chimney," I'd plead, "but I can't always hit it!"

Looking back and considering the amount of plaster I knocked loose, it's a marvel we kept any pictures on our walls. More marvelous still, that I was permitted to continue my backyard activities!

Sometimes I tossed the ball up on the roof and tried to catch it when it rolled down again. That never became an obsession with me because too often I had to retrieve the ball from the gutter around the roof by a long reach out the upstairs bathroom window.

A better practice area was in front of our house where a cement walk led up to big stone steps. It was ideal for rebounding grounders. Still, there was always the danger of hitting the edge of one of the steps and sending the ball ricocheting onto the porch, against the siding, or into the screen door. When that happened, I'd draw another complaint from inside.

At 5:30 P.M., I knew Dad's 1937 Chevy would be pulling into the yard. I never failed to be there waiting for our daily ritual. Regardless of how tired he was or how anxious to get inside, take off his shoes, and get ready for supper, he never refused to join me in the backyard and "throw a few." Sometimes he hit some pop-ups for me. And always there were words of encouragement about my progress.

The best place for batting practice was the Richardson Marble and Granite Works where my father was owner and manager. The shop was always filled with odd-shaped marble and granite fragments chipped off in the process of making tombstones. I'd fashion a bat out of a one-inch strip of wood, round the handle a bit, and scatter rock chips all over the lot in back of the shop. As I did, I played an imaginary game, trying to bunt and advance the runner, shoot through the infield for a base hit, and, of course, come up with a grand-slam home run whenever necessary.

As I grew older, the elementary-school yard, only a block from my house, became more and more important. There I'd hit and field with any of the other boys who wanted to play and I'd keep at it until their interest flagged.

There too I met Harry Stokes, a high-school student at the time, and during the summer a player in the American Legion baseball league. Like most boys who love baseball, Harry was drawn to the sight of youngsters learning to play. While passing the schoolyard one day, he offered to hit some grounders to the half dozen or more youngsters playing there and we, of course, were delighted. I knew him at once as one of the town's outstanding second basemen. I'd seen him in action on many nights when Dad had taken me to the Legion games at Sumter's Riley Park. Before many sessions in the schoolyard, Harry became my idol.

I was eight years old at the time, and when I discovered that he lived only two blocks from my home I couldn't resist the temptation to pay my hero a visit.

Harry tells the story of awaking early on a hot July morning after a baseball game the night before and finding a small boy, chin-high to the bed and wearing a baseball cap, staring at him.

"Good morning," Harry said, thinking me a relative, perhaps one of his small cousins. He was too sleepy to comprehend that a nonrelative would come to the door so early and wander upstairs for an interview.

"Harry, I want to play baseball," I said.

"Sure, we'll do that sometime."

"But I want to play *now.*"

He came up on one elbow and tried to focus on the clock beside the bed. It was 7 A.M. He fell back on the pillow. "I'm going to get up after a while," he said.

When Harry awoke again, it was 10:30 A.M. and I was still standing there. He gave up.

"O.K. Wait till I get my clothes on."

After dressing, he went outside and played catch with me for a few minutes before going to the kitchen for coffee.

That was the beginning of a friendship that was to ground me in the essentials of baseball and nearly pester Harry to death. I became his shadow and sought him out early and late. Because my childish interest in the game matched his more mature interest, he overlooked the years of difference in our ages and devoted hundreds of hours to teaching me everything he knew.

He became a regular visitor at our house where he and my father found a topic of mutual interest—my development as a player.

Both Harry and Dad were excited when I reached my tenth birthday and was old enough to play on a baseball team sponsored by the Salvation Army. That was my first experience on a squad and because all the other boys were older, bigger, and could throw and hit harder, there was some doubt about my making the grade.

Fortunately for me, most boys of this age don't enjoy climbing into a catcher's heavy equipment and crouching behind the plate. Wearing the big mask and all the padding is like being one degree removed from the action. It's much more exciting to be out on the pitcher's mound, around the infield waiting for the hot grounders, or even in the outfield where you can make a dramatic sprint and snag the long fly ball. I had no special love for heavy equipment either, but I cheerfully volunteered for catcher when it appeared it was my only chance to be on the roster.

Special permission from my parents had to be secured because the Army team played away from home quite often. There was no regular season schedule; pickup games were arranged by phone, sometimes only a day or two in advance. Then we piled into cars, journeyed to nearby towns, and played any team made up of boys in a comparable age group.

The permission of my father was a foregone conclusion but the approval of my mother was another thing. She was troubled by thoughts of my youth and questions of how much the strenuous playing might affect my health (she had read somewhere that youthful athletes needed more rest than other children). So it was agreed that I would lie down for a set period before each game. I can still remember dashing home from school so that I could get my rest period out of the way quickly and go to the diamond.

There was some amusement when I appeared at the first game. In the rustle of equipment behind the plate, it was hard to spot the team's smallest member. But we had a good season and I picked up valuable experience in ball handling. Heavy equipment or not, no player on the diamond has to deal more often with a ball in flight than the catcher.

The next team I played on was an entry in the Knee Pants League, a YMCA baseball program similar to Little League. Once again I found myself the youngest and smallest player and again installed behind home plate.

My father came to every game I played in. He usually sat in some inconspicuous bleacher seat instead of the grandstand. While he enjoyed himself, he never cheered or rooted. He just sat, solemn and composed, absorbing the action and keeping his thoughts to himself.

Nothing was quite as encouraging to me as seeing Dad and Harry seated together, watching the game, or spotting Harry's wave of encouragement after a tough play. I needed lots of encouragement in those days because I was sensitive and a poor loser. Every defeat suffered by our team was my personal tragedy and I was in the depths of despair for hours afterward.

Why had I bobbled the toss to the plate when the runner was sliding home? If I had gotten off my throw to third more quickly, the stealing runner would have been nailed. Why couldn't I get more wood on the ball when up to bat? On and on.

It seldom occurred to me that the other players had hitting and fielding problems. I was too immersed in my own problems to notice.

Meanwhile the long practice periods with Harry continued in the schoolyard after classes and on Saturdays. Sometimes, when a light drizzle or a cold wind emptied the yard of the other boys, Harry and I would keep on—not for an hour or two, but all day.

Our favorite workout was a pepper game in which he hit grounders and, 8 or 10 yards away, I'd pick them up. When it grew late or Harry was tiring, he'd say, "As soon as you catch 100 straight, we'll quit for the day."

He still insists that I'd drop one on purpose somewhere between 90 and 100 and we'd have to start all over again.

I couldn't keep back the tears when the weather was too bad for us to play. Nothing Harry or my father could say made me feel any different. They didn't argue with me because they felt the same way about the game. They knew it took an interest like that to make a major leaguer. Interest and a few other things.

"He's good with the glove. Real good!" Harry would say.

My father would nod, then the two would fall silent while I knew what each one was thinking—"*But he's small at the plate!*"

It was undeniable. I *was* small. And it takes more than a good glove to play major league ball. It was a worry the two men seldom expressed but it was a worry that would be with me for many a long year.

3

Finding Time to Play

DURING THOSE YEARS my life had a simple purpose: finding more time to play. In school mathematics captured my attention but in many other classes I found my imagination taking me outdoors. How could I cut some time off my paper route in order to play longer before supper? Would there be time at recess to play three innings? If I got to be captain, whom would I choose to pitch, play first, shortstop, outfield?

Maybe that was one reason I stayed out of trouble in school. When other boys had spitball fights and fired erasers across the classroom, I thoroughly enjoyed the horseplay without joining in. Then, when those boys were kept in from recess, my enjoyment continued outside.

The only time I was sent to the principal's office was when another boy was caught copying my paper. I couldn't understand it when they told me that was as bad as if I'd done the copying. The other boy was bigger than I was, and if he wanted to copy my paper I was going to let him!

My first job was the delivery of 125 newspapers after school. Because most of them went to subscribers who lived in apartment houses, I honed the time down to 11 minutes flat.

But there was simply no way of improving on the long, dreary job of collecting each Saturday, wasting hours that might have been spent playing ball, standing in doorways while subscribers fished through their pockets for change or burrowed around in dresser drawers, wallets, and sugar jars.

I managed to eliminate the problem of homework by digging in and finishing everything in study hall. I can't remember many nights during elementary and high school when I brought books home from school.

This isn't to say that I ended up as class valedictorian. I didn't. And I could have learned a lot more if I *had* taken more time and studied at home. I know now that I should have. But in my mind, then, I majored in sports. Everything else was a minor.

I wasn't interested in the theory behind sports, either. Not a bit—only action. Even when my father took me to older youth league games at night, it was a mixed blessing because *I* wasn't out there playing.

On many occasions my one compensation for being stuck in the bleachers was the fact that I knew second baseman Harry Stokes. Harry went directly into semi-professional ball upon graduation from high school and played on the Sumter team of the Palmetto League. Dad and I were sure to be in the crowd of two or three

Top: The family that makes home-coming such a joy—my wife, Betsy, and our four children, ...nie, Ron, Christie and Robby. (PHOTOGRAPH BY LOUIS REQUENA.)

...ottom: With my sisters, Inez and Ann—always loyal fans of mine.

Top: The day I was born he said, "Someday he'll be in the major leagues." My mother and late father, Mr. and Mrs. Robert Clinton Richardson, Sr.

Bottom: The Sumter American Legion team in my high school days really gave me a boost in baseball (that's me, front row, fourth from the left). (PHOTOGRAPH BY B. L. MC GRAW.)

thousand people turning out for Sumter's home games.

I spent a good bit of my time in the bleachers telling all the kids within hearing distance that the man on second was a personal friend of mine. Naturally I was a little crestfallen and embarrassed when he made no response to my yells, and after one game I said, "How come you don't speak to me?"

"Robert," he explained, "I can't talk to you when I'm out on the diamond."

"The least you could do is touch your hat when I yell."

"O.K. O.K. I'll touch my hat. But nothing more!"

Harry claims that was his big mistake. Twenty or thirty times each game, he'd hear a shrill voice from the sidelines, "Hey, Harry!" and when he touched his cap, there was a roar of approval from the small fry in the area where I sat.

The other players on his team began to notice. "Boy, what a crowd-pleaser!" they'd tell him in the dugout. "How about a little concentration on the game, Harry?" "Say, fellas, I think Harry's growing rabbit ears!"

He finally made me promise not to yell more than once each inning.

My long-suffering idol found relief when his team traveled. I'd accompany him and they'd let me sit in the dugout when his team was up at bat. There I'd bend his ear discussing the various plays, talking strategy, and analyzing the opposition pitchers. But at least the stands were quiet.

Meanwhile the long practice sessions with Harry continued and I settled down to a steady berth at shortstop in the Knee Pants League. Occasionally I pitched.

Once I had a strep throat and the doctor said baseball was absolutely out until I recovered. He must have been impressed with my doleful expression because he relented and agreed to let me attend an important game. But it was understood that I was to be present as a spectator *only*.

On the night of the game, my mother rehearsed all the warnings and instructions of the doctor as Dad and I prepared to leave. To ease her fears, Dad delayed our departure until after the game had started.

I wore my baseball uniform and sat with my father. Our team, sponsored by the Kiwanis Club, fell behind and some of the boys asked if I could be allowed to play. I can't remember exactly what my father said but suddenly I was in the game, plugging away for the honor of the Kiwanis Club. When we finally won, it seemed to be well worth the effort.

I don't recall the scene at home afterward, either. Perhaps, by that time, my mother had given up the hope that I would act sensibly in anything connected with sports.

Baseball was a regular undercurrent in our family life. Dad loved to listen to "Game of the Day" on the big Philco beside his bed. He'd urge me to listen too. But before long, I'd get itchy and wander outside for a ball-toss against the chimney.

Some days we'd all pile into the Chevy and drive into the country. Nearly always, Dad had to visit some rural cemetery and at a customer's request sketch the style or copy the wording on an old tombstone. Afterward we often ranged far and wide through the woodland, sometimes hiking several miles before coming back to the car and heading home.

The first time I remember seeing a major league game was when my father took a carload of boys over to Columbia where a Yankee Class B team (I don't remember which one) played against the Cincinnati Reds in an exhibition. I remember Dad pointing out Yankee Frank Crosetti after an outstanding play. "Keep your eye on that shortstop," he said in his enigmatic way. And I did. I didn't learn until much later that my father envisioned *me* playing in that spot for the Yankees.

On another occasion Dad took a carload of boys to Columbia to see the St. Louis Cardinals play the Cincinnati Reds in an exhibition. Stan Musial was the talk of the boys all the way over, and after the game they joined the crowd outside the dressing room to get Musial's autograph.

I remember a strange sense of embarrassment. I really didn't want his autograph—I just enjoyed seeing him play.

"You mean you don't *want* Stan Musial's autograph?" the kids asked.

I shrugged and flushed. I couldn't explain it then. Later I knew. The real excitement in baseball is in the game, not the personalities. I admired Musial as much as the other boys did, but I didn't want his autograph. I just wanted to play *the way he did!*

Although baseball occupied most of my time and thought, I was also interested in a number of other sports, all sponsored by the Sumter YMCA.

At the Y, I found men any boy could look up to because they combined physical prowess with Christian conviction. Ed Garris, Jim Lollis, Charles Nooney, Jack Nantz, and others influenced me for good during the years of my development as an athlete.

I looked up to men like them because, in a game of touch football in the YMCA gym, for example, they'd join right in. And they were always the ones able to fade back and toss the long pass or run to the other end of the gym and catch one.

It was more, though, than the admiration of a small boy for the physical skills of someone older. On Sunday I saw those same men on their way to Sunday school and church, their Bibles under their arms.

Perhaps because they were able to make all sports exciting for young boys, I found myself enjoying tumbling, table tennis, kickball, football, and basketball in addition to baseball.

Many people are surprised when I tell them I am as interested in basketball as in the sport I've given most of my life to. But most professional athletes have another sport competing for their interest. It's not at all uncommon to come across a group of professional baseball players enthusiastically talking about basketball games they've played. Or pro basketball players talking for hours about baseball, golf, or bowling.

I played my first basketball game at the Sumter Y when I was ten. I remember the game because we lost 37-1, with my next-door neighbor and close friend Sonny Husband making the only point for our side. One reason we lost was a swift-footed guard named Jim Beattie on the opposite team. That was several years before Jim became one of the world's top milers.

The YMCA had a full range of teams for all ages—the Mites, Midgets, and Juniors. I played every year, and in 1949 the end of the season found me on an all-star team heading for Elkin, N.C., for the YMCA Regional Basketball Tournament.

Both Dad and Harry were disturbed. They knew the tournament would make me late reporting for baseball practice at high school. Since I was a freshman, I already faced the disadvantage of competing with boys already established at their positions on the team. But I had no intention of playing basketball all winter, then passing up an all-star tournament.

Dad and Harry never quite understood my interest in running around indoors and trying to toss a big, fat ball through a hoop. But they bore with me patiently, and when I turned up two weeks late for baseball practice they crossed their fingers.

Maybe I'd be lucky and pull off a big double play.

Maybe I'd stroke a long ball past the outfielders during batting practice. Maybe the coach would overlook my small size and be impressed with my hustle.

No go.

I reported on the first cut-down date and was dropped from the roster the same day.

4
A Flame is Lit

THE MOST IMPORTANT day of my life came in my fourteenth year. It came when baseball was my biggest interest. It came unexpectedly, and for a long time afterward I didn't realize the importance of what happened.

The pastor of Grace Baptist Church, the Reverend J. H. Simpson, came to call at our house. That in itself wasn't unusual. The minister, a slow, quiet-speaking man of deep sincerity, was a regular visitor of his members. But on that day as he entered our home his eyes sought out Willie Ann, Inez, and me. He knew us by name as he did all the children of the church.

Before long we knew that he had come to talk particularly to us.

As we sat down in the living room, appropriately subdued and serious, I realized that I didn't know him in a personal way. I was used to seeing him behind the pulpit on countless Sundays, perspiration standing out on the top of his head where the hair was getting scarce, and his eyes behind the glasses gleaming with intensity as he proclaimed the gospel.

Now, as he sat looking at the three of us in the intimacy of our living room, I was impressed with the quality of love that endeared him to everyone. I remember most vividly the impression—*He's really interested in me!*

His purpose on that day was simple: to explain to us the Bible's plan of salvation. I'd heard it many times. It was the theme of most sermons and it was outlined again and again in Sunday school lessons. But on that day it was different.

Mr. Simpson used the best-known verse in the Bible to make salvation plain—John 3:16: "For God so loved the world, that he gave his only begotten Son, that whosoever believeth in him should not perish, but have everlasting life."

All mankind was sinful and in need of God's mercy and salvation. Did we know—Willie Ann, Inez, and I— that we too were sinful? No one had ever put the question to me directly before, and it caused some self-examination.

Was I really sinful? Certainly I hadn't thought of myself that way.

If someone had asked me if I were a Christian, I probably would have said "yes"—not a first-rate one but certainly better than average.

I'd gone to Sunday school and church for as long as I could remember. It was the accepted thing to do in my family.

I must admit that I enjoyed Sunday school more for its social aspect than for its spiritual value. Most of my friends were there. And I liked the group singing, the choruses, the learning of Scripture verses, and the ritual of dropping pennies, one for each year, into a big missionary jar, whenever it was anybody's birthday.

Generally, I managed to keep out of trouble most of the time. My worst offense was sassing my mother occasionally. But when she became sufficiently aroused, I was whipped and the matter forgotten. My disobedience usually took the form of going out to play after I'd been told to clean up my room. Or showing up at seven o'clock when I'd promised to be home at five. It didn't occur to me to call that "sin."

Of course, there were times when, down deep, I wondered if things were really right between the Lord and me. I knew, for example, that there was something different about the Sunday school teacher who taught my class when I was fourteen. Bill Ward was a plain and simple man who lived on a farm near town. There was no pretense of any sort in him. He said exactly what he meant and he punctuated his words with "Praise the Lord!" He probed and pushed and questioned the high-strung, mischievous boys who were his responsibility every Sunday as though that were the only way he could communicate the love of God he knew in his own heart.

Maybe that was why he insisted that each boy take a turn and teach the lesson. I know that made me dig into the lesson a lot deeper—knowing I had to stand up before the others and talk about it. And before I'd been a student of Mr. Ward's for very long, I was enjoying my first taste of public speaking. But I sensed that our instructor was looking for something else, something he hoped would emerge from our teaching experience.

I knew there was something different too about one of the boys in my class, Dickie Alderman. It wasn't just that there was a real zeal and enthusiasm when he talked about the Lord or that he knew so many Scripture verses by heart. I noticed him at noon in the school cafeteria, bowing his head and praying unashamedly over his lunch. Something inside of me responded to him. I worked hard at memorizing Scripture but there was still a fundamental difference that I couldn't put my finger on.

At the conclusion of each Sunday morning church service, Mr. Simpson extended an invitation to accept Christ. Evangelists visited our church from time to time and they too extended invitations at the conclusion of their messages. Although we were asked to bow our heads in prayer, I often stole a look or two and saw other boys raise their hands, indicating their desire to be Christians, and go to the front of the church to show their faith publicly.

Many times I wanted to raise my hand too and go forward. It was like an inner wrestling match. Something seemed to be pushing me forward while something else was holding me back. I resolved the struggle each time with the thought that I *was* a Christian—I *did* believe in Christ. The invitations were for others, not me.

Once I did raise my hand. Phil Saint, the gospel artist, was concluding an evangelistic service at Sumter High School. I was there with others from the junior high school and was deeply moved by the message. I raised my hand, thinking that the speaker was calling for re-dedication of life, then pulled my hand down hastily when he explained that his invitation was to those who had not yet accepted Christ as Saviour. Once again there was turmoil within me. If I was such a solid Christian, why was I disturbed by these invitations? If I really knew Christ, what else could I be looking for?

Those thoughts flashed through my mind as Pastor Simpson sat in our living room that day and asked us quite simply if we believed that we were sinners in the eyes of God. It was a penetrating question. God's Word said we were. He read Romans 3:23: "For all have sinned, and come short of the glory of God." *All.* That included me. I didn't feel particularly sinful. I didn't feel particularly like classifying myself that way. But the pastor had put the Word of God before me and I could believe it or not. I chose to believe it.

"Yes," I said, "I'm a sinner."

He went on to explain that we are not sinners because we sin. We are sinners by birth, by nature, because of

Adam's fall. Some sin more, some less, but all are sinners, separated from a holy, righteous God. We cannot blame God for this because He has provided a wonderful way out of the dilemma.

God loved the world so much that He sent His Son Jesus Christ to do for men what they could not do for themselves. Jesus lived a perfect life and in His death on the cross made the perfect sacrifice for the sins of all the world. God's love met all the requirements of God's justice. And as men voluntarily believe in Jesus and submit to Him, His shed blood *really does* blot out all their sins and they can stand without fear or shame in the presence of God's holiness.

Those facts were not new to me. What was new was hearing them from someone who told me *face to face* that *they applied to me!* I had believed without difficulty that Jesus had died for the sins of the whole world. But had He died for *my* sins? It was quite a different question.

Once again my answer came and this time I would spend the rest of my life discovering its importance.

"Yes," I said, "Jesus died for me."

My sisters gave the same answer. The pastor bowed his head and asked God to bless us. Then, after instructing us to read our Bibles regularly and to pray, he left.

Mother had gone on with her duties in the kitchen with purposeful silence. Now the house was quiet as we found normal conversation hard to resume. I caught a glimpse of myself in the hall mirror. I looked the same. Inwardly I felt the same. There had been no great emotional experience. I picked up a baseball, tossed it from hand to hand, found the familiar urge to play was still there. In the days that followed, there was no startling change that anyone could observe in my life.

School seemed the same. There were no radical changes in my relationships at home, with friends, on the ball diamond. My personal conduct neither worsened nor improved greatly.

I tried to follow the pastor's suggestion about daily Bible reading. I started out bravely in Genesis, bogged down in Exodus, and finally gave it up.

In view of those things, *had* anything really happened to me? And if so, what?

A clue was in the way I prayed. For years I'd knelt each night by my bed and recited,

> Now I lay me down to sleep.
> I pray Thee, Lord, my soul to keep.

Not all at once, but little by little, starting around that time, I dropped that recitation and began to talk to God. He became personal.

There would be a "lull" of several years before I would experience any real spiritual growth. But I know now, looking back, that in the living room of my home that day, in the simple act of believing that Jesus died for me, the power of God's Word began to work. I saw, for the first time really, that a live, flesh-and-blood Person had suffered an agonizing death because of love for a boy named Robert Richardson.

In that moment a tiny flame of desire was kindled in me, a desire to know this Man, to follow Him, to show Him my gratitude. And though there have been detours along the way, that flame has never gone out.

5

High School

THE FOLLOWING SUNDAY my sisters and I and a number of other young people came to the front of the church following the morning message. We made public confession of our faith in Christ, and formally requested baptism.

In the manner traditional in our church, the congregation by voice vote said "aye" to our being accepted as members. It seemed to me, even then, to be too "easy." In all the time I'd attended church, I'd never seen a person publicly refused membership.

The feeling of tradition seemed to me to cloud over the real significance of our public confession and to take away from its spontaneous quality.

However that was forgotten as I looked into the beaming face of Pastor Simpson. Later, at the close of the service, when we stood with him at the front of the church, I saw in the face of Bill Ward the real significance of what we had done. He was the first to reach me, his hand gripping mine warmly, and his "Praise the Lord!" expressing real joy.

For a while during that period in my life, I began to think it would be pretty wonderful to be a minister. My father had no comment on that idea, probably feeling mixed emotions, but mother was delighted.

I found that I enjoyed talking about the Lord and was quite ready to tell of how I'd accepted Him into my life. But my doubts about going into the ministry centered around my hesitancy in personally challenging others to make a similar commitment. Through the years this has been a persistent source of condemnation. While some others found it easy to approach people, I found it hard. I was tormented with thoughts that I was trying to force my experience on others. I valued my own privacy too highly to wish to be guilty of that. On the other hand, I knew that my own conversion was a direct result of a personal challenge.

In later years I came to depend more completely on God and less on the instruction books about personal evangelism. If there is someone God wants me to speak to in a personal way, I depend on Him to let me know about it and to give me the words to say.

However, at fourteen, baseball continued to absorb most of my attention and a good share of my waking hours. After failing to make the high-school team in my freshman year, I kept working out with Harry and getting ready for the American Legion tryouts. Sumter Legion Post No. 15 ran a summer team for boys from fourteen to seventeen years of age and I was eligible.

Tryouts started the week after school closed and I was

one of the first who reported to Riley Park for opening practice.

Legion ball has always been popular in the south, and Sumter, together with Orangeburg and Greenwood, had a habit of winning. Competition started with four teams vying for an area championship. Then came lower state, state, regional, sectional, and Little World Series. Quite often these three South Carolina towns managed to send teams to the upper brackets of championship play. For this reason it was considered an honor to make the Sumter Legion team and a number of good players turned out, including high-school team members, fresh from their twenty-game season.

That was the first time I'd had to compete for a position. In Salvation Army baseball, I was catcher because nobody else wanted the spot. And in Knee Pants League, if too many boys turned out they simply formed a new team. Everybody played.

Add to the competition in Legion ball the fact that I was fourteen, small for my age, and shy of the faster pitching. I leaned away from the big curve balls and as a result hit the ball softly, collecting a fair amount of base hits but rarely driving a long one for a triple or homer.

"Hutch" Hutchinson, coach of both the Legion and high-school team, thought I looked good enough to make the grade, so after the cut-down dates and to the delight of Dad, Harry, and myself, I was installed at second base.

I had a pretty good season. Although I seldom hit with authority, I walked, bunted, and depended on my legs to get on base and keep moving. The long hours with Harry paid off on defense. Although most of the other players were seventeen, my glove work was up to par.

The whole team had a good year and at season's end we found ourselves in Charlotte, N. C., playing against a team from Richmond, Va., for the sectional championship. One more win and we'd go to the Little World Series at Omaha.

It was there that I got my first taste of big game tension and the bitterness of losing out on a close and important play.

A couple of thousand fans from Sumter had driven up to Charlotte for the game and I knew that thousands more were listening over the radio.

In the eighth inning, with the score 3-3 and a man on first, a Richmond player shot a ground ball to short. I took the relay throw at second base and fired over to first for what looked like an easy double play. The Sumter fans went wild, then hushed as the second-base umpire ruled that my foot hadn't touched the bag. That made the advancing runner safe at second, and he went on to score what turned out to be the deciding run.

Suddenly I was the goat of the game instead of the hero. I still remember the roar of angry disappointment from the stands. But what could I do?

After the game I poured out my grief to the one I

knew would understand. "Dad, I stepped on the bag. I really did!"

He put his arm around my shoulder and in his quiet way, said, "I know, son. You've never lied to me."

In spite of the disappointment, it was after that game that I had my first contact with a major league scout.

"I can't talk to you legally," he explained, "but remember my name. I'll be back when you graduate."

He was observing a rule set by the Commissioner of Baseball that scouts may not attempt to influence or bid for the services of a prospective player before the boy is out of school. It's a good rule but it doesn't change the excitement when a real, live scout comes over to a high-school sophomore and shakes his hand. And it doesn't stop a boy—or his father—from dreaming.

It was about that time that I became interested in major league games. It was the year the Phillies won the pennant. I started what was to become a lifelong habit, turning each day to the sports section of the newspaper. At World Series time, I rooted for the Whiz Kids, hoping the Yankees would be beaten. Instead, to my disappointment, the Phillies were whipped, four straight. Not until I signed with the Yanks did I give up rooting for their "underdog" rivals.

When tryouts were held for the high-school team during my sophomore year, I didn't have much trouble winning a berth at second base.

That spring the Yankees arranged for one of their

farm teams, Norfolk of the Class B Piedmont League (managed by Mayo Smith), to hold spring training in Sumter. It was quite a thrill to see those players work out and to realize that each man was driving hard to find a place on the parent club in faraway New York City.

When school closed, I resumed my shortstop position on the Legion team and began to see more of Mr. Smith. The Norfolk team worked out during the day in Riley Park and the Legion team held its home games on the same field at night.

Mayo and the Norfolk business manager, H. P. Dawson, came out to many of our night games because the Yankee top brass were interested in our big first baseman, Julian Beard, a lefthand-throwing, righthand-hitting player who was one of the brightest prospects ever seen in Sumter. A number of scouts were interested in him. I learned later that Mayo noticed me while keeping vigil on Beard.

Although we were eliminated on the district level that year, I was learning a lot of fundamental baseball from Coach Hutchinson—the double steal, hitting behind the runner, bunting runners over, the hit-and-run, etc. I've always been a "thinking" player, trying to anticipate the action, but then I was getting acquainted with the more intricate offensive and defensive plays that make baseball challenging.

I was building confidence, too. I stopped worrying about the curve balls and the brush backs. I knew I could trust my reflexes to keep me out of trouble. That meant I could stand in there and swing harder. Although I struck out more often, I began to connect for more doubles, triples, and homers.

Legion ball isn't the best place to become a specialist. When games were close, I often found myself switched from second to short or third. And on more than one occasion, I pitched. But the quality of competition was good and I learned to appreciate the limitations of each position on the infield.

I also learned from Hutch the value of hustle and team spirit. He played the game from the dugout with as much fervor as anybody on the field. And he was always a gentleman. During my years under his coaching, he was thrown out of games three times, accused of using improper language. But nothing could be further from the truth than such charges. His favorite expression when aroused or frustrated was "Dad Bum!" —which had nothing at all to do with his opinion of the umpire.

About that time Harry Stokes was drafted into the army. We didn't know it then, but the two years away proved to be his undoing as far as a career in baseball was concerned. When he returned, he'd been out of active competition for a good while. Life had moved on.

6
Signing Up

I MISSED HARRY and wrote him often at his training base in Fort Jackson, S.C. I knew many boys who were interested in baseball but no one with Harry's patient endurance who would play pepper with me in the schoolyard until it was too dark to see.

I missed him especially in the fall of my junior year. That was when I took a part-time job in a recreational center about ten blocks from my home. The center was operated by the town and my task was to organize games of volley ball, kick ball, baseball, and football for the boys after school.

Although I included myself in some of the games, I had much less time to play, and in addition had to attend night meetings of the boys' club that was a part of the center.

Spring baseball came none too early for me that year, but when it did arrive the season was made brighter by the fact that my friend, Sonny Husband, made the team as a pitcher. He'd made the team the year before, then broken his arm before the first scheduled game. This time he had other problems.

Coach Hutchinson made it a rule that players were not permitted to drink water during practice. He believed water drinking cut down on a player's efficiency. Another Hutchinson belief was that running would solve practically any problem a boy might have in getting into shape.

Sonny simply couldn't get it through his head that he could run without water. As a result he carried a small bottle in his back pocket while he pitched, and as he turned back to the mound he'd whip out the bottle and take a quick snort behind his glove. He was expert at it and, as far as I know, completely fooled the coach. Seeing our pitcher acting like a confirmed alcoholic, however, convulsed the rest of the team and he was given a good ribbing. But he was very serious. To Sonny, water on a hot day was no laughing matter.

After a good season on the school team, I entered my third year on the Legion team and at summer's end we'd played through the various divisions of competition to the sectionals in Charleston, S.C. Here we were finally stopped by a team from Austin, Texas.

Scouts from twelve major league clubs expressed an interest in me at Charleston but by that time my hopes were fastened on the Yankees. Earlier in the spring Mickey Owens, new manager of the Norfolk team, had invited me to work out with the team one day at Riley Park. And after that, signing with the Yankees had become my chief hope.

However, Spud Chandler, a Yankee scout who was at Charleston, had doubts about me. He didn't think I could make the shortstop's long throw to first out of the hole between second and third. He called me a good, little aggressive infielder but too small for major league ball. At that time I weighed 158 pounds and stood 5 feet 8 inches high. *Too small!* I'd heard it for years and I'd hear it again!

While others in the Yankee organization had doubts too, H. P. Dawson of the Norfolk club was sure enough about me to pay a visit to my father and make arrangements to sign me on the afternoon of my graduation from high school.

Knowing this, the days, weeks, and months of my senior year at school dragged by. I sat in class and tried to imagine what my life would be like when there were no more classes. It seemed impossible that I would actually leave my hometown and begin a career in baseball! When something has been dreamed about for so long, it's hard to believe when it finally happens.

The day arrived at last, and in our living room at home—with Dawson, my mother, father, and sisters looking on—I penned my signature at the bottom of an impressive-looking document that made me an official member of the Yankee organization and put my foot on the first rung of a ladder leading to big league play. I was to find out before long that the ladder was crowded and climbing would be tough.

After signing, things began to happen fast.

Fred Heath, owner of the Coca-Cola franchise in Sumter, offered me a free, four-day trip to New York City to meet and work out with the Yankee major leaguers. Heath was part owner of a Sumter baseball team that participated in the Tri-State League, an independent Class B league. He had a special interest in me as a Sumterite and in the Yankees because he "borrowed" farm league players for his club whenever the Yanks had a surplus of young signees. Lee McFail, then Yankee farm director, was glad to have a Class B club he could use to keep all his prospects in action.

Heath had a private plane but I showed some hesitation about traveling north that way—I'd never before been aloft—so the two of us took a train to New York City on a sunny morning about a week after graduation.

Coming from the quietness of Sumter, I was shell-shocked by New York. As our cab fought its way through the midtown traffic on the way to the Bronx, I stared, marveled, and hung on for dear life.

"Boy, I sure don't want to ever live here!" I remember thinking.

Traffic was forgotten, however, when I first caught sight of the vast expanse of Yankee Stadium towering over the Harlem River, its highest deck rimmed with flags cracking in the wind. Home of the World Champion New York Yankees! Home of a club where American League pennants and World Series championships were a proud tradition! And *I* was a Yankee—even though hardly anyone knew it outside a small town in South Carolina!

Here for the first time I could see the men I'd seen only on television or in the newspapers—shortstop Phil Rizzuto, third baseman Andy Carey, second baseman Gil McDougald, and the likes of Berra, Mantle, Bauer, and Ford.

Mr. Heath introduced me to Manager Casey Stengel and to a number of the staff members. Most were friendly but busy. Then I went to the locker room to change. I must have cut a comic figure because Frank Crosetti, then a Yankee coach, noticed my battered baseball shoes and said, "Hey, kid! You can't wear anything like that. Here! This looks better!" And he handed me a brand-new pair of cleats, the most beautiful pair of shoes I'd ever seen—and they were just my size!

"But they're yours!" I protested.

"Forget it! They're yours now!"

It was a big honor to participate in the pregame workout with the regular Yankee squad and I admit I was a bit edgy. Normally I'm nervous before a game, not with pregame jitters but simply because I'm anxious to play. But then it was different.

I was grateful when Phil Rizzuto, Jerry Coleman, and Gil McDougald came over and shook hands with real friendliness. It took away some of my stiffness and I took my turn at batting practice without freezing up. Watching the crowd filing into the giant stadium, I tried to imagine what it would be like to be a major league regular warming up for a game with a pennant or a world championship at stake.

After I'd showered and changed, I went upstairs and showed Mr. Heath my new shoes. He was aghast.

"Why they're worth twenty dollars if they're worth a nickel!" he said. He pulled out his wallet and handed me a twenty. "You take that right down to him, Robert. We can't let him do a thing like that!"

I had the feeling it wouldn't do any good. And it didn't. Crosetti was indignant. "I didn't *sell* you the shoes. I gave them to you!" he said.

Back I went to Mr. Heath with the report of Frank's reaction. My hometownsman could do nothing but let the matter rest. But he wouldn't take the twenty back. "You keep it," he said.

So I put the twenty in my wallet. How could I complain? I'd gotten a pair of new shoes plus the twenty dollars the shoes were supposed to be worth!

I was permitted to participate in two of the pregame practices and to enjoy grandstand seats for four major league games. Then we were on our way home. I honestly don't know whether or not Casey Stengel ever really noticed the short player in the shiny new shoes who worked out with his crew before two of the games that spring. But I was determined to draw his attention sooner or later.

I was hardly back home when it was time to leave for Norfolk. Dawson's glowing report had resulted in something pretty unusual. Right out of high school, I was going to report to a Class B club! It was a big jump to skip Classes D and C, but there it was. I would be joining the very team that held its spring training sessions in Sumter.

I was silent as Dad and Mother drove me to the bus station. Going off to New York had been exciting and there had been a lot of laughter and jokes. This was something else. I was going away from home *to live.* And I didn't feel much like joking.

I remember wondering, as we pulled into the bus station, why so many people were there. But then, maybe somebody'd had a family reunion or a group was departing for a church camp somewhere. *But a remote unit from the radio station!* Just then, I spotted Harry Stokes hurrying toward me, a big grin on his face. I noticed Mother and Dad were grinning too. Then that whole crowd was clustering around, congratulating me, shaking hands, wishing me luck. I was overwhelmed.

The radio announcer came over, pulling his lines from the sound truck, and I tried to think of some appropriate remarks. Mostly I just stared around at all the smiling faces of friends, neighbors, coaches I'd worked under, boys I'd played ball with—and I felt like crying.

Harry made a speech in which he covered me with glory. Then I was presented with one hundred dollars in cash, and a pen and pencil set.

A big cheer went up as I climbed aboard the bus. As I sat down and looked out at the crowd—still waving, still shouting, "Best of everything, Robert!" "Show 'em you're from Sumter!" Keep in touch, Bobby!"—I felt a big lump rising in my throat.

What could the Yankees offer me that could match this?

My mother was mopping her eyes with a handkerchief. "I can hardly believe you're really going," she said just before I climbed aboard.

As the bus started to pull out, I wanted to run to one of the exits, jump off, and shout, "Don't cry! I can't believe it either! I'm going to stay!"

But I didn't. I just sat there, fighting that lump in my throat all the way out of the Sumter station and far down the road to Virginia.

7

The Awful Fifteen Days

MY BUS LEFT Sumter near 6 P.M., and arrived in Norfolk at 5 the next morning. Because of the excitement and the fear of dozing through my stop and waking up in Houston or Los Angeles, I didn't sleep. As a result, I was dead tired when I stepped off the bus in the pre-dawn at the Norfolk Greyhound Terminal.

Amidst all the preparations for going away and all the speech-making about a wonderful career in baseball, nobody had given much thought to what was actually awaiting me in Norfolk. I'm sure my parents simply took it for granted that when I arrived everything would be taken care of.

As a matter of fact, nobody was there to meet me. No provision had been made for where I would stay. All I had was the name of the business manager of the club, H. P. Dawson, and the address of the ball park.

What a letdown! When I left Sumter the night before, I was the town hero. The next morning in hustling, sophisticated Norfolk, I was Mr. Nobody.

Standing there in the bus station for a few tired and bewildered minutes took a lot of the shine off the idea of a career in baseball. Until that time, I'd thought only about playing. Now I'd suddenly come up against the other side of professional sports—living away from home, finding a room for yourself, making out on your own.

Finally I picked up my suitcase and moved out to the sidewalk. A neon hotel sign glowed in the dusk a few blocks away and I headed for it.

It was a funny time to check in, but I signed the register and was taken to a room. I phoned the desk to request a call at 10 o'clock, climbed into bed, and fell asleep.

When I awoke, I didn't feel a whole lot better but at least the sun was up. After I checked out, I had breakfast at a nearby cafeteria and caught a cab to the ball park.

I'd timed it so I'd get there about the time the first players arrived. I knew the name of the Norfolk Tars manager, Mickey Owens, and eventually I tracked him down. He'd been expecting me and introduced me to several of the players who were getting into uniforms in the locker room. Especially friendly were second baseman Herb Plews and pitcher Leo Perrent. I asked where most of the players lived and they offered to take me after the game to their rooming house where they thought a room was available.

Top: The first pitch of the 1960 World Series, with Hal Smith catching.

...ter: Betsy and I flew to Tokyo for the thrilling New Life campaign in February, 1962— ...r learned to write my name in Japanese, though. (PHOTOGRAPH BY JAPAN AIR LINES.)

...om: The Japanese youngsters I met during the New Life campaign were a lot more ...y than the American youngsters I was used to. I surely enjoyed meeting them.

Top left: At the end of the season, packing up my equipment to leave Yankee Stad
and that smile wasn't just for the photographer!

Top right: Yogi had been a fine player, and as manager led us to the Pennant in 196

Bottom: Tony Kubek and I admire Mickey Mantle's Most Valuable Player award for
Mickey was always the spark plug of the team even when, as in 1963, he played under
physical handicap.

As more players arrived, there were more introductions and a lot of banter at the expense of Dick Sanders, the shortstop.

"Here's the boy to take your place, Dick!" "Hope you can get your job back when we see you again!" "Hey, Dick, if you're late getting back, don't worry about it! We're all fixed up at short now!"

Sanders was about to leave for three weeks of Marine Reserve training and I'd been sent to take his place. It was funny and yet not so funny. The Tars were having a hot season, the pennant was a real possibility and Dick Sanders was leading the Piedmont League in home runs.

As it turned out there was nothing for Sanders to worry about.

I was awed by the field. The Norfolk stadium was the biggest I'd ever seen, subtract Yankee Stadium, and it was a whole lot different from cozy Riley Park.

I felt nervous and out of place and repeatedly bobbled the ball or shot over the first baseman's head. But the real trouble came at bat. That's when I knew right away that something was wrong. I'd never faced pitching like that in high school, Legion, or anywhere else. The fast balls were *fast* and the curves were fast too—and tricky. I drummed out a .150 average while at Norfolk, popping up, beating the ball into the dirt, striking out, and occasionally running out a single.

After my first day, we found there was space available at the rooming house. Five dollars a week gave me a room of my own and a one-third interest—along with

Herbie and Leo—in a bathroom. Because it was several miles from the ball park, we rode back and forth in Leo's old DeSoto.

"You'll snap out of it!" Herb told me when I complained about my batting and fielding.

"What do you expect, coming in here in the middle of the season?" Leo offered.

In spite of their sympathy, I had the kind of sick feeling you get when you're doing your best and it's not half good enough.

Of course there were excuses—if you wanted excuses. I'd come fresh out of high school into a fast-moving Class B ball club in midseason. The pitchers in the league were warmed up and good. The teams were running smoothly and pennant fever was on. I simply wasn't the man to jump into the middle of the Norfolk infield and take the place of Dick Sanders.

The fans found it out right away. They missed the team hero and were critical of the nervous, young-looking replacement from down-country. After I struck out three times straight, the boos started, and kept building until my appearance at the plate signaled a barrage of derogatory remarks from the sidelines.

"Hey, Richardson, this isn't Little League!" "Who's going to change the baby's diapers?" "Send him back to grade school!"

That really shook me. I'd never run into that kind of reaction from fans, had never been booed in my life. And the treatment didn't improve my fielding, either.

The Awful Fifteen Days

Twice as tense, I fought a losing battle for control. I'd either take too long to make sure my peg to first was good or I'd fire fast and wild, making the first baseman dive away from the bag.

It was tough on the field but it was worse when the game was over and I was gloomily eating supper in some restaurant, or sitting in my room, reliving my mistakes of the afternoon. It was a relief when Sunday rolled around and Herb invited me to a Methodist church he attended in downtown Norfolk.

Each new day at Norfolk made me more homesick, and almost every night I'd call home. It was comforting just to hear the voices of my mother and father on the other end of the line. But it was expensive.

After several nights punctuated with long phone calls, my mother gently hinted that I call a little less often. At that my father exploded in one of his rare bursts of anger. Calling me back, he instructed me to phone any time, from anywhere, and talk as long as I wanted.

I'd never enjoyed being away from home. When I was eight years old, my father took a long weekend off, an almost unheard-of event, and drove us all to Savannah. I moaned and groaned all the way down, and when the family went for a dip in the ocean I refused to go near the water. The plan had been to visit relatives in Savannah, go swimming, and do some shopping. But I made everybody so miserable that finally, after we'd been in Savannah only a few hours, my father drove us all back home. It was a 300-mile round trip and when we pulled into Sumter late that night nobody was happy but me.

My homesick phone calls from Norfolk may have been a contributing reason in the decision of my folks to pay me a visit. It was cheaper to drive up than to talk to me long distance. Of course there were other reasons too: they'd be able to pay a visit to my mother's brother at nearby Virginia Beach and commute to the park each day to see me play.

I was happy about their coming, and at the same time I dreaded it.

It was about that time when a letter came, one of the most important I've ever received. It was from Conley Alexander, a physical education director at Sumter Junior High School. He'd been out of touch with me for several years since our association in school, which made the letter and its timely arrival even more significant.

It was a simple letter of encouragement in which Conley expressed his pleasure that I'd signed with the Yankees. But he added a word of caution. Professional baseball, he wrote, is a matter of ups and downs. Don't let baseball—or anything else—stand between you and God. And he quoted Matthew 6:33: "seek ye first the kingdom of God, and his righteousness; and all these things shall be added unto you."

The letter recalled the decision I'd made in our living room at home when I was fourteen. It reminded me that

I was a Christian, a person with a different set of values and a different kind of destiny.

Had I forgotten that in the years since I was fourteen? Had success in sports during high school obscured it? I don't know. I do know that reading Conley's letter in those discouraging days at Norfolk made me aware again of the small flame that had been lit years earlier—the flame of desire to know and follow Jesus Christ.

It was wonderful to see my family when they arrived, but humiliating to strike out, ground out, pop up—knowing Dad was in the stands, knowing his pride in me. I knew he was stunned by my poor performance and the way the fans sounded off. Of course, he didn't say anything—nobody did—but that made it even harder. The family stayed at Virginia Beach and each day Dad would drive in for the afternoon game, whether anybody else did or not. Afterwards I'd ride back with him for supper, then return to Norfolk the next morning.

I found out later that the general manager of the club met with my father and discussed the problem. Mr. Dawson said that I was simply outclassed, and Dad agreed. Dad didn't say anything about their talk until the two of us were called into the office one day and I was told that I was being sent down to a Class D club. Mr. Dawson was very kind and Dad told me it was nothing to be ashamed of. Still, I was deeply disappointed.

So much had been written about the fact that I was

starting with the Yanks on a Class B level. *Now* what? Flash-in-the-pan! After fifteen days at Norfolk, the big pink bubble had burst. And what about Harry and all the folks who, only two weeks earlier, had sent me off with cash, gifts, and speeches?

I guess I wasn't listening very intently when Mr. Dawson told me where they were sending me—Olean, New York. *Where?* Later, when they gave me traveling instructions, I was handed train, bus, and ferry tickets. I was told that Olean was farther north than New York City. My heart sank. Norfolk had seemed relatively close to home. Olean seemed like the other end of the earth.

I was dead sure I wouldn't like it.

8

Johnny Hunton

WHEN I FINALLY arrived at my new assignment, I was pleasantly surprised. Olean was a town about the size of Sumter, the people liked the ball club, and the players were about my age, most of them recently out of high school.

On the field I was pleased, too. Although my arm was still erratic, I wasn't the only one with problems. Best of all, I could stand at the plate and *see* the balls again. I got the range and began to hit.

Although I played in only 32 games, I finished the season with a .412 average and went back to Sumter in high spirits. Norfolk was beginning to seem like a bad dream.

I enrolled at the University of South Carolina in their business administration course. I had a grand plan to combine higher education with professional baseball and the schedule called for picking up one semester each winter. Over a period of six or seven years, provided I took a heavier course load than usual, I'd end up with a college degree right in the middle of a major league career.

But it didn't work out that way. As it stands now, I'd never advise a boy to pass up or postpone a college education in order to play minor league ball, because it's too risky. I don't have the percentages but I know that the proportion of boys who start out at the bottom in professional baseball and make it to the top is very small. Unfortunately it often takes years to discover whether you're actually going to make it or not. In the meantime you may get married, start a family, and all of a sudden college is too difficult to handle.

My advice is this: go to college as soon as you can, following high school. If you have a scholarship, use it. If you can play ball in college, do it. Baseball in the larger universities is often on a par with Class B professional ball, and the experience will be valuable. With your degree behind you, and given an opportunity, you can get into professional ball. And if you don't make it, you've got a fine education to fall back on.

In my own experience, I found that I didn't like my first semester at the university and never went back. The math was interesting, as always, but the other courses—literature, history, sociology, and such—were on a tougher level than high school and I'd never developed good study habits.

I was glad when February finally rolled around and I could think of baseball instead of books. Because of my performance at Olean, I'd been picked with twenty-four other rookies from the Yankee farm system to attend a special instructional school at St. Petersburg. That was Casey Stengel's brainchild and was held ten days before regular spring training began for the parent club. The idea was to accelerate the progress of promising rookies by giving them an intensive workout under the eyes of Casey and key members of his coaching staff.

Although we tried to treat it lightly and "professionally," all of us were excited and the competition in the intersquad games was rugged. In the mind of each of us was one thought: here's the chance to jump all the way to the top.

George Sternweiss, a former Yankee second baseman and a one-time leader in American League hitting, had been hired to work with the infielders. That's when I found out the top brass had decided to take me out of short and make me into a second baseman.

I didn't mind going to second as long as I could play. But there's a real difference in the positions. At short, you have less time to knock down the ball, get control of it, and fire over to first. And your throw, often a long one, has to be fast as well as accurate.

At second, you have that extra fraction of a second to work with. You can get the ball on the bounce or have a little trouble with it and still get it to the first baseman in time. The motions and limitations of the second-base position are different than short but speed is still necessary, especially when you're trying to pull off a double play.

Although I've never bent any manager's ear about

this, I've always liked the shortstop position better. I like the added challenge of charging the ball in the deep hole and getting off that long, powerful throw across the diamond in time to cut off the runner.

I must say this, though: as long as there's a Tony Kubek at short, or anybody with his ability, I'm content at second.

In St. Petersburg that spring, I was returned to the position I'd played in high-school ball. But I was taught how to be a miser with every motion, how far to move from the bag with a righthand hitter, a lefthand hitter, when a bunt was on, when the bases were loaded.

I learned how serious is the double play in professional baseball. The runner advancing from first has one duty: to disturb the peace at second base so that the ball doesn't get away to first on time. This disturbance can come at you hollering and shouting like a lunatic on the loose, or like an attacking mountain lion, his back in the dirt, claws up. Either way you have to concentrate on the ball, tag the bag, make your throw, then get out of the way of the runner.

Sternweiss taught me too how to move up on grounders, cover another base when necessary, and how to go to my right, backhand the ball, and still get it over to first in time.

Casey concentrated on making us into "thinking" players. After hours of fielding practice, he'd pepper me with questions:

"Where do you stand when there's a runner on first?"
"Why?" "What if he starts to steal?" "What do you do
in a run-down?" "Why?" "When do you cover for the
shortstop?" "Why?" "What are the dangers?"

It was at St. Petersburg that spring that I first met
Tony Kubek and Ralph Terry. There weren't a lot of
close friendships developed during these ten days, however, because each boy was bearing down hard, learning
all he could, trying to demonstrate that he had the stuff.

In spite of the fact that there was a lot of hard work
packed into that short time, and all the boys seemed to
me to do quite well, none was honored with an invitation to stay on for spring training with the parent club.

On the final day I was assigned to the Yankees Binghamton, N.Y., club and traveled to Orangeburg, S.C.,
only 60 miles from Sumter, where that club was beginning spring training.

Binghamton was in a Class A league, and in spite of
my Norfolk experience the Yanks were again gambling
that I'd be able to skip several steps in the ladder.

Here, too, at the Class A level, I began to run into a
different sort of atmosphere among the players. Although there were always the enthusiastic, hard-playing
boys, I found others who had grown cynical and bitter
from long years in the minors. For them the romance
and excitement of the game had disappeared. Foremost
in their thoughts was the fact that they hadn't made it to
the majors. As a result they regarded each promotion

with a jaundiced eye. "How come *he* was moved up and not me?" "That's politics for you." "Just treat the right people right and you get the breaks."

I found out too that no one was going to rush out a welcome mat for a youngster fresh from Class D ball.

I managed to win a regular position at second base and was thrilled when I found that we were scheduled to play an exhibition at my hometown before heading north. Sumter declared "Robert Richardson Day" and a huge crowd turned out at Riley Park to see me play against the team I had failed to stick with—the Norfolk Tars!

We won in a landslide but I went 0-for-4. Everybody else on our team had a great day while I went without a hit. For some reason it's been that way every time I've been singled out for special attention.

During spring training in Orangeburg I first heard about Johnny Hunton. There was a rustle of excitement one day when the news was passed around that Johnny, who had been playing Double A ball with Birmingham of the Southern Association, was being sent down to our club. He'd played for Binghamton before and most of the oldtimers knew him.

"Watch out for this guy," I heard them say. "He's a preacher!"

"We better fix up our language, fellas. Hunton's coming back!"

"If he corners you, he'll convert you before you know what's happened!"

I got a mental picture of a wild-eyed fanatic, but when Johnny finally arrived I found him to be a quiet and likable fellow and an experienced infielder who could play all the positions. He was forthright and open about his Christian convictions. He bowed his head for prayer in restaurants, regardless of who was present, and he carried his Bible without shame—but I have never seen him try to cram his faith down anybody's throat.

As a matter of fact, at Johnny's arrival that flame in me—smoldering and small—began to burn brighter. For the first time I began to see that it was possible to be a professional baseball player and an uncompromising Christian at the same time.

Together with Buddy Carter, our third baseman and also a Christian, I'd go to churches where Johnny was invited to speak during the baseball season. I admired his courageous and unashamed stand for Christ and wished I could speak with the same boldness.

He was married and often invited me to supper. There too I was impressed. Instead of simply offering a short prayer before eating, Johnny read from the Scriptures, then discussed with his wife what message God had for them in the verses. I saw the kind of Christian marriage that was possible in the midst of a baseball career.

When our team was on the road, Johnny carried his Bible and never let anything interfere with his time of devotions. At that period in my life, I was addicted to movies, and whenever I had a free night or rain washed out our game I'd hightail it to the nearest theater featuring a western. But I noted that Johnny made time in his schedule for a long walk, a quiet time alone, and a period of personal Bible study.

I saw the quality of his life on the playing field too. Although an experienced player, he was made a utility infielder while I found a regular berth at second base. But it made no difference in our close friendship.

When he struck out, he didn't throw down his bat, argue with the umpire, or stomp to the dugout. He'd come back, take his seat beside me, grin, and say, "I'll get him next time!"

He was exactly the same player when he was hitting well as when he was deep in a slump.

One highlight of that year with Binghamton was an exhibition we played with the parent club. The big league players arrived by bus and were given a police escort to the ball park. The newspapers gave the event a lot of publicity and our enthusiasm was at a fever pitch. We were convinced that our visitors were determined to play as they'd never played before. (I learned later that a major leaguer's reaction is something like this: "What? Another exhibition with a minor league club! Oh, no! Let's try to get out after the second inning!")

My heart beat faster when they jogged out onto the field, the men whose names filled the sports section of the newspaper every day—Mickey Mantle, Yogi Berra, Billy Martin, Gil McDougald, Phil Rizzuto.

Mickey hit a mile-long homer over the center-field

fence that day, but when the smoke cleared we'd whipped the pennant winners, 5-2. To my credit were a couple of good defensive plays and a double into left field off pitcher Bob Weisner.

The next day a newspaper columnist quoted Stengel at some length, including a comment on the Binghamton second baseman. "You've got a boy here that might do us some good one of these days," the old man of baseball was supposed to have said.

I soared to Cloud Nine.

9

A Taste of Major League Action

THAT FALL, WHEN I returned home, I enrolled at Clevenger Business College in Sumter and signed up only for those subjects of special interest to me—business law, accounting, business math, etc. I went to classes in the morning and after 6 P.M. worked in a local gas station. In between I hung out at the YMCA, played basketball, or went dove hunting.

On Sundays I attended Grace Baptist Church and it was there that I first became aware of Betsy Dobson. The pews in the church sanctuary are laid out in the form of a big C around the pulpit. As a matter of habit I sat in a pew to the preacher's right. Across the sanctuary, in plain view but about the distance from third base to first, sat a girl with her mother—same place every Sunday. Our eyes met occasionally but I looked away quickly to avoid seeming too bold. Still, as Sunday followed Sunday, I wondered how I might meet her. My side of the sanctuary emptied out one exit and the people on the other side left by another exit. Hope of an "accidental" meeting at church seemed remote.

I found out later that the same thoughts were running through her head. By sheer coincidence we both decided to do something about it on the same Sunday. Immediately following the benediction, I quickly started to cross the intervening pews in order to go out Betsy's exit. At exactly the same moment, she headed my way with a similar intention. We nearly ran into each other midchurch and were so embarrassed we mumbled "hello" and hurried on in opposite directions. Once again we left the church by different exits.

A week or so later I was with Sonny Husband and spotted her at the County Fair, an event held annually in Sumter. I also spotted Robert LeNoir, a young man I'd heard had once coached Betsy in softball, and I asked him if he could—just casually—arrange an introduction. Blessed with quick understanding and fine tact, he managed to work out the whole thing in the next few minutes.

I couldn't think of much to keep the conversation going, so before long Betsy and the girls who were with her said, "Nice-to-meet-you," and disappeared into the crowd. Several moments passed before Sonny said, "Why don't you ask her to go on one of the rides with you?"

I started to come unparalyzed. Why sure! Why hadn't I? Leaving Sonny with his mouth open, I charged off into the crowd, looking for Betsy. But I'd waited too long. By that time she was high in the air on the Sky Ride, or Ferris wheel. I'd lost her.

Next came a football game. Sonny and I were broke, so we waited at the ticket gate for half-time when we could get in free. Betsy's brother-in-law, Oscar Strange, (whom we knew) saw us standing there and offered us two extra tickets he had. When we gratefully accepted and joined him in the stands, there was the girl I'd lost in the crowd at the fair.

Neither of us ever would have won a prize for boldness, so we exchanged a minimum of remarks during the game. However, I felt that at last I could call her up and ask for a date.

Our first outing together was at a miniature golf course. I didn't realize it then but Betsy had been a hard-playing tomboy, for all her feminine looks, and as we neared the end of our round together she was leading me by 7 points. Betsy relates that about that time she recalled advice given her by an older girl to the effect that a girl should never beat a boy in sports if she were trying to impress him. Her game fell off sharply then, but in spite of everything and to her own dismay she came out 1 point ahead.

If I needed further evidence that ours was no ordinary date, Betsy told me later in the evening that she was a Christian and asked me point-blank where I stood with the Lord.

She recalls her fear that I'd never date her again. As usual I kept my real feelings well hidden. But after I took her home that night, I knew I'd be seeing her much more often.

Although I've never been able to carry a tune, I signed up for the church choir and afterwards took Betsy home. She became my companion at church and sat with me on the preacher's right. I was invited to her home where we popped corn in the evening, listened to records, talked about the Bible.

Because of a .310 average at Binghamton, I was chosen again to attend Casey's "instructional school" in the spring. Parting with Betsy was difficult and after each day's drill in St. Petersburg, I wrote her.

There was some talk that I'd be invited to stay on for spring training with the parent club but nothing came of it, and when the final day arrived, I was assigned to the Triple A Denver Bears of the American Association.

The thin air at mile-high Denver was a shock. During my first few days, running out a double would have me huffing and puffing at second base. But within a week I was used to it, and even liked it. The pitchers had trouble making their balls break, and when I connected with one it seemed to soar farther.

We felt we had a real advantage when visiting teams came in and struggled through a three-day series. But the advantage quickly disappeared when we went on the road and played at normal altitudes.

Coach Johnny Pesky, former infielder and manager of the Boston Red Sox, took me under his wing and spent a lot of extra time showing me the fine points of batting.

At St. Petersburg, Casey had noted my habit of hitting "straight away" and warned that they'd run me out of the major leagues unless I quit it. Now Johnny went to work to eliminate it. He taught me to get quicker wrist action so that I could "pull" the ball into left field or delay a fraction and "push" a shot into right field.

Up to that time I'd taken a cut at the ball with one idea in mind—hitting it. As a result, most of my hits occurred with the ball about even with me and ended up in the vicinity of center field. I saw how outfielders might easily peg me as a "center-field hitter" and crowd over to pick off every fly. I had to learn to push and pull the ball to keep those outfielders spread out. It was important with ground balls and liners too in order to keep the third baseman "honest." If he began to creep over toward the pitcher, I'd have to be able to pull the ball down the baseline.

I had a good season at Denver, batted .296, and it was a big thrill when Manager Ralph Houk called me into his office in August and said, "I've got good news, Bobby. The Yankees are calling you up. I hope you stick and the next time I see you is up there!"

Happy as I was at going, I knew Ralph meant just what he said. He too was aiming for an active position at the top and he'd spent many more years waiting for it.

Before becoming a manager, he'd spent nine years on the bench as a back-up catcher for Yogi Berra.

I'd been called up suddenly because Gil McDougald had been hit by a line drive in batting practice, and my first full game as a player in a major league game was a night game against the Detroit Tigers in Yankee Stadium. I walked out on the field and looked around at the biggest crowd I'd ever seen in my life—65,000 people! I was fresh from Denver where 15,000 was tops.

There are two reasons I'll never forget that game: first, I got a base hit, stole second, then came in on a homer by Mantle; second, I never touched the ball on defense.

I would have been more relieved if I'd booted the ball. But as it was, I waited, inning after inning, for a grounder, a pop fly, a liner, a slow roller—anything. I waited for the first defensive play of my major league career—and nothing came near me. I left the game a nervous wreck.

After that fair start offensively, however, things went downhill. I had my first taste of real platooning, Casey Stengel's specialty. If I started in a game, I'd be pulled out almost immediately as a pinch hitter was sent to the plate in my stead. If I did get to bat once in a game, I was so tense that I tried too hard. Often I was sent in as a pinch fielder in the game's last innings.

On the other hand, who can blame Casey? With a bench full of proven major league power hitters, why would he send in a rookie with one hit for seven times at bat?

I confess that the logic of this argument escaped me when, nineteen days later, I was sent down to Richmond. I knew the club needed some pitching help from the minors, and I knew the roster had to be opened to permit this; Gil McDougald was back in the lineup, and I was the logical one to step down. But it's never a happy occasion.

I took the long train ride to Columbus, Ohio, where the Richmond club was currently on a road stand and shared my woes with pitcher Jim Konstanty who'd been sent down with me.

I'd rather have gone back to Denver where Ralph Houk and my Denver friends were enjoying a winning season. Instead Jim and I were on our way to join a club exactly 42 games out of first place.

When we arrived, my disappointment sharpened. The team's morale was completely shot. Everybody was waiting for the season to end. Batting practice and pregame drills were skipped most of the time. And the crowds were so poor that some of the staff members whose salaries were tied to the gate receipts, had been broke for weeks.

I'd been promised a berth at shortstop but the one man on the team having a good year was the man on short who was batting near .300. They weren't about to pull him out. So I took up my familiar duties at second and tried to make the best of it.

I played for 20 days, appreciated seeing action every day, and batted .286 before the Yankees called me back up. By then the parent club had captured the pennant and I played in eleven games as Casey rested up his regulars for the World Series.

Called up too late to be eligible for Series play, my mind had turned back to Sumter. I'd had enough ups and downs for one year. And when the annual baseball classic was on, I was deep in the South Carolina woods dove hunting.

It's a strange fact that baseball players rarely enjoy a baseball game on television, although they'll watch with interest a basketball or football game on TV.

Of course, all players are interested in the results of games. And I had a special reason to be interested because that year the Yanks voted me one third of a share of their World Series money. It amounted to about $1,500 and verified what I'd known all along: the Yanks are just about the most generous club in the country.

That winter I worked at a service station and during my time off got to know Betsy better. On weekends we played miniature golf, went to football games, and were a regular twosome at most church services.

Although the idea scared me a little, I must admit that marriage had been on my mind for some time. I think the idea shakes up most bachelors when they first think of it seriously. Anyway, I wanted to foresee her reaction to a proposal, so one day I asked if she would accept a ring from me. I didn't actually state that it was an engagement ring but, serious as anything, Betsy accepted. She said she would keep it but wouldn't wear it because she felt it was a little too early to be formally engaged. When I told her I had no ring, she flared up in one of her rare moments of anger. I couldn't understand why because it had been meant as a kind of joke.

We were both very much in love and it held us together in spite of stunts like that on my part. Leaving for St. Petersburg in the spring of 1956 was tougher than ever as I headed for my third straight year at Casey's school.

Ralph Terry and Buddy Carter were there again; also Jack Reed, who went on to become a Yank reserve outfielder; and Mickey Mantle's twin brothers Ray and Roy. The latter two were bigger than Mickey, just as fast, one a righthand hitter and the other a lefty. I thought they were the best prospects in camp and envisioned an all-Mantle outfield for the next 10 to 15 years. But so much was expected of these two from the public, because of the name they bore, that they labored under a severe disadvantage. Eventually both left baseball.

That spring I was kept on for spring training with the parent club and went north for the opening of the regular season. I felt that I'd made the grade at last. All I needed to complete my happiness was Betsy as my bride. And before that happened I'd have to actually propose.

I invited Betsy and her mother to come to New York, and one day soon after their arrival I took Betsy's hand and said we were "going shopping." Somehow she got the idea that I was proposing marriage when I took her into a jewelry store and asked her what kind of a diamond ring she liked best.

It was one of those places off Fifth Avenue, recommended by some of the fellows on the club, where you can get all kinds of jewelry at a discount—if you're willing to take your chances. That afternoon, an unseasonably cold, blustery day in late April, Betsy, her mother, and I walked all over town getting that ring appraised until we were satisfied that it was all the seller said it was. That settled, Betsy and I were officially engaged and agreed that midsummer was an ideal time for her to come north to New York as my wife.

Then my major league bubble popped again. A few days after Betsy and her mother had departed for Sumter, Casey called me into his office and handed me orders to report to Denver.

10

Earning a Place
in the Lineup

WITH THIS DEVELOPMENT I decided to marry
Betsy right away. When I reported to Denver, I went to
club owner Bob Howsan and asked for some extra time
to get married. He was indignant.

"I should say not!" he glowered, "I've never heard of
anything so ridiculous in my life!"

Next I appealed to Manager Ralph Houk.

"Sure thing," he said. "How much time do you need?"

"A week."

"Go ahead."

My phone call to Betsy must have been a real shocker.
She'd been home wearing my engagement ring only a
few days when marriage was suddenly two weeks away.
A few phone calls, some hasty preparations, a meeting
with the Rev. Knox Lambert, pastor of Grace Baptist
Church in Sumter, and we were standing in the sanctuary of the church making the most serious vows a man
and woman can make to each other and before God. My

close friend, the Reverend Dickie Alderman, assisted in the ceremony.

As it turned out, we were wed only five days before my draft board issued a call. Five days later and I'd have been off to basic training instead of Denver.

There was no time to waste before setting out on the long drive west, and three days later we pulled into the capital city of Colorado. I had just time enough to pull one more of my "jokes." When I spotted a ramshackle and abandoned house in the outskirts of Denver, I pulled into the yard.

"Well, here we are! Home sweet home!"

Betsy swallowed, looked out the car window, then put on a brave smile.

"I expect we can fix it up right pretty."

Then on we went to the apartment I'd arranged for, and while she got things straightened up I reported to the field. Gene Hassel, the Bears' second baseman, had been hitting a towering .390 but the orders from New York were firm: put Richardson in. I was tremendously impressed with Gene's attitude about stepping down in the middle of such a big season. He went out of his way to make things pleasant for me, even surprised me by waxing my car one day. This kind of spirit is rare in baseball or anywhere else in life.

I had a good year at Denver, and picked up a lot more confidence and experience. (I can prove statistically that marriage did me good. I was hitting at .250 just before our wedding but finished the season with a .328 average.)

Back home that winter, we stayed with Betsy's mother. Mrs. Dobson owned a large piece of land about 20 miles from Sumter and I began to hunt quail there with a dog owned by a friend, Buck Jackson. Quail hunting became a steady off-season activity that provided fresh air, good exercise, and real relaxation from baseball.

The rest of my exercise was found in basketball at the YMCA where I participated in pickup games or refereed contests between younger boys.

There was no exercise in the job I picked that winter. I was a salesman in a Sumter clothing store, and I found out quickly that salesmanship was not for me. I shied away from the idea of actually taking money from a customer for a suit. What if he got home, looked in the mirror, and decided he didn't like it? With that sort of attitude, it's understandable that I dropped the job by Christmas.

I went to spring training with the New York team in February and fought hard for a position. But it was like swimming up from the bottom of a lake to get a breath of air and finding a foot-thick layer of ice over the water.

These were the tried and proven veterans in charge of the Yankee infield:

Phil Rizzuto—"Mr. Shortstop," for several years voted the Most Valuable Player in the American League. Although not a big guy, he was a tremendous fielder and a consistent hitter.

Andy Carey—a third baseman who had racked up several over-.300 seasons at the plate, an excellent fielder with amazing reflexes at the "hot corner."

Billy Martin—sparkplug of the whole Yankee team, aggressive and tough. Versatile infielder and a dependable clutch-hitter.

Jerry Coleman—smoothest infielder in the American League. Made all the difficult plays look easy. Could play second, short, or third.

Gil McDougald—a power hitter at the plate and defensively a great student of batters, played the deepest second base I'd ever seen and made every play in the book without difficulty.

It wouldn't be hard to imagine talent like that developing a "private club" atmosphere and resenting an upcoming rookie. But every one of those players gave me encouragement. Jerry Coleman, especially, spent hours with me, perfecting my pivot move, showing me how to charge slow rollers, and helping me eliminate my skip and jump in the double-play maneuver.

I was grateful to be taken north with the club that spring and breathed a big sigh of relief when cutdown day arrived and departed and I was still in New York.

Betsy had gone to spring training with me but had stayed in Sumter for the birth of our first child, Robert III in early June. He must have had a stimulating effect on me because one day I hit Billy Martin on the nose with a bad hop grounder during batting practice, and while he recuperated on the bench Casey put me into Billy's spot at second base. McDougald had moved over to take Rizzuto's place at short while Carey was at third base.

My batting average climbed over .300 and the other players began to razz Billy, calling him "Wally" and asking him about his headache. That was a reference to Wally Pipp, a Yankee first baseman who, one day in 1925, developed a headache and asked to rest on the bench for a day until he felt better. A youngster named Lou Gehrig went in as substitute and 2,130 games later was still playing.

Billy took all the kidding in fine style and came back with some of his own. He threatened to put "something" into my orange juice, load my car with a time bomb, and once asked in all innocence, "Got any mail from the government lately?"

"No," I said.

"That's funny. I wrote your draft board more than a month ago!"

Casey appreciated my performance at the plate but missed Billy's verbal vinegar at second base. Even the sports writers began to poke fun at the perfect silence that reigned in the Yankee infield. McDougald, Carey, and first baseman Skowron weren't noted for their noise-making abilities and I was likened to "Long Bob"

Meusel who reportedly said no more than "hello" at the beginning of the season and "goodbye" at the end.

Billy was Casey's idea of a real "holler guy" and the old man never quite resigned himself to the fact that I wasn't cut out of the same cloth. Still, he gave me a lot of help, and made me sit by him in the dugout while he discussed the various pitchers.

"See that Bob Lemon there," he'd point out. "Watch how low he throws 'em. He's trying to get the batter to beat those balls into the dirt. You gotta let those throws go by, make him get the ball higher where you can get a hold of it!"

When Early Wynn was pitching, he'd point out Early's habit then of keeping the ball too high, trying to lure the batter into an easy pop up.

Most hitters like the ball a little high where they can get as much benefit as possible from the power in their shoulders. I do, myself, although I usually have trouble with the high inside fast ball.

Casey reminded me again about "pulling" the ball into left field and "pushing" it into right. He'd pointed that out in St. Petersburg and Johnny Pesky had worked with me on it in Denver, but frankly it wasn't needed in Triple A ball. Hitting straight away and hard was all I needed to pass muster at Denver. But it wouldn't do in Yankee Stadium. The opposing outfielders were too wise.

This illustrates a key difference between major and minor league ball playing. In the majors, there's that extra alertness and the instinctive knowledge of what to

op: Tony is a terrific guy to start the double play, as Joe Cunningham and a host of others
d out the hard way.

wer left: One of the first lessons I had to learn was concentration—don't worry about the
le; be oblivious to everything but that ball and the play. This was a fly-ball hit during the
inning of the game with the Cleveland Indians, April 27, 1963. (UNITED PRESS INTERNA-
AL PHOTO.)

wer right: Citations like this one, the Red Shield Award of Merit from the Salvation
y, are sobering as well as exalting. (WIDE WORLD PHOTOS.)

Top: The dugout is the seat of some long thoughts as well as many a practical joke—here with me are Phil Linz, Yogi Berra, and Elston Howard. I wonder if Phil has a harmonica in his pocket?

Bottom: Judge Sam Phillips McKenzie presents the Lou Gehrig Memorial Award from Phi Delta Theta. Charlie Berry, Chads O. Skinner, and Rev. Charles L. Copenhaver look on.

do when a righthand hitter comes up, a lefty, a hitter known for his bunts, a hit-and-run artist.

In the minors you usually find two, maybe three out-standing players on a team. In the majors, everybody is good. In the minors, one or two good pitchers. In the majors, there's never any letup. Tough pitching is your steady diet.

In the majors you bang out a ball that at Denver or Richmond would have gone through for a single—but in Yankee Stadium the infielders come up with the ball.

Minor league pitchers most often try to throw past you with their fast ball. In the majors, they don't throw any harder but they *want* you to hit the pitch they serve up. They want you to get just enough wood on it to foul, pop, ground out, or hit into a double play.

I decided early in my career not to be a gambler and try to "outguess" the pitchers. Some batters do it with various degrees of success. But it's also possible to enter-tain a hunch that a curve is coming, then get your block knocked off with a high fast ball.

I guessed only once and quit while I was ahead. It was in a game at Kansas City and the Yanks were having a tough time with the Athletics' pitcher that day. All but me, that is. I had 3-for-3.

In the dugout, Mickey sidled up and said, "How come you're hitting so easy against this guy?"

"Simple," I told him. "He makes a certain move every time he gets ready to throw a curve."

"Don't say anything if you don't see his sign," he told

me, "but if you see he's going to throw that curve, yell my name."

I watched from the dugout as the pitcher threw a couple. Then I spotted the characteristic motion. "Come on, Mickey!" I shouted.

Mantle swung and hammered the ball into the street behind the right-field fence.

Trotting into the dugout after his round trip of the bases, he paused, shook my hand, and said, "O.K. That's one I owe you."

In the midst of my hitting honeymoon in the summer of 1957, the veteran infielder Billy Martin was traded to Kansas City. The transfer came as a real blow to him and it stunned the rest of the team.

The night of the trade the Yankees sat in their bus outside the Kansas City ball park waiting to leave for the hotel, and nobody was talking. Billy was the last one to enter the bus. We could see his eyes were reddened as he made his way down the center aisle. There were plenty of seats available but he went all the way back to where I sat alone and eased in beside me. Gripping my hand, he said, "Good luck, kid. Don't worry, you've got it made. You'll be around a long time!"

It was a gallant gesture from a great ballplayer and I've never forgotten it.

Earlier that year there had been a lot of talk about trading me to Cleveland in exchange for pitcher Ray Narleski. Naturally I had no desire to leave the Yankees and was greatly relieved when the trading dates passed.

Trades are important and necessary in baseball but often they exact a costly toll in a player's emotional life.

When Casey picked me for the second string on the 1957 American League All-Star Team, I thought life couldn't be more complete. Then one of those totally unexplainable things happened: I slumped. From something over .300, I went down to .256 and before long found myself back on the bench with Coleman installed at second.

Casey had a wait-and-see attitude about my hitting all along. Would the major league pitchers eventually discover my batting weaknesses and plow me under? For a while, in the latter part of the '57 season, it looked that way.

Glum as I was about my slump, I had to admire our manager. Eccentric and unpredictable, he earned the respect of all the players. Casey would take the team apart in a clubhouse meeting. He'd rant and rave, and if he had reason to get on some individual he did it in front of everybody.

He jumped on me once about my habit of swinging at the first good pitch. Casey thought I ought to take more strikes. "You can't get many walks if you're a first-ball hitter," he'd say. After I tried his way unsuccessfully for a while, he looked over at me during a subsequent meeting and growled, "Just forget that taking business; you were better the other way!"

He used me occasionally in the latter part of the

season—starting me, then pulling me out for a pinch-hitter, or sending me in late in the game. My average didn't improve. Some of the sports writers were beginning to chant the good-field-but-no-hit ditty about me again. But to Stengel and anybody else who brought up the question, I had the same answer.

"I have to play regular to do any good at the plate."

It didn't help me that I pulled a hamstring muscle near the end of that year. Although I could play, my leg was slow in healing and I favored it.

Bench-warming has always been tough on me, and after a while I'd do almost anything to relieve the monotony. I finally went to Casey and offered to work as a bullpen catcher. I was grateful for the exercise, and far from Casey's eagle eye I could talk, play word games, and otherwise relax when there were no pitchers warming up.

Of course there was always the danger that unexpectedly I'd be called into a game I'd stopped paying attention to. That's exactly what happened one day. The bullpen phone rang and it was Casey with the word that I should hurry over to first to pinch-run.

I noted the runner on third but in my haste overlooked the other runner on second. As the pitcher went into a long windup, I saw a golden opportunity to steal. The fans screamed "No! No! No!" and just in time I saw the startled runner on second. I skidded to a stop and raced back to first, making it just in time. Casey stared from the dugout. Some of the players observed that his face and mine were about the same shade of purple.

These mental lapses happen even when you're trying to be careful. Hank Bauer tried to steal second with the bases loaded during a game at Detroit. It was in the eighth inning with the score tied 4-4 and I was on second, Bill Skowron on third.

Suddenly I looked up and here was big Hank barreling down the base path toward me. He stopped halfway, saw his mistake, and tried to get back. He seemed hopelessly trapped but Skowron and I danced off our bases trying to attract attention. Fortunately the pitcher made a weak throw deep to third base, permitting Skowron to score what turned out to be the winning run with a diving headfirst slide for home. The third baseman saw there was no play at the plate and tagged me out instead.

The 1957 season drew slowly to a close with the Yanks again pennant winners. After playing me in the first inning of the opening game against Milwaukee, Casey put in Jerry Coleman who did a fine job at second base.

My dad was disappointed. He made the long trip north to attend his first World Series but saw me at bat and in the field only once.

In Sumter there was even more disappointment. Betsy's grandmother, then nearly 80 years old but stimulated by the success of her granddaughter's husband, had purchased a television set. When the games were telecast, she permitted no interruptions. All through the latter part of the season she sat in front of the set watching every inning and rooting enthusiastically, "Come on, Robert! Get another touchdown!"

Her knowledge of the game was limited but she was one of my most ardent supporters. And when she learned that Casey had decided not to use me in the Series, she refused to watch the annual classic—and wouldn't let anyone else view it over her set! Betsy's Aunt Jenny, who lived with Granny, had to go down the street and watch the contest on a TV set owned by a neighbor.

II

Learning to Hit Hard

"WHY DO YOU play baseball on Sunday?"

That question was asked again and again that winter as more speaking engagements came my way. Earlier, at Norfolk, I'd accepted Sunday baseball without much thought. Now, in prayer, I brought the whole matter before the Lord again.

My mind turned back to a Sunday school teacher of mine at Sumter and a fine Christian gentleman. I remembered that occasionally he missed his class on Sunday morning because, as an employee of the Carolina Power and Light Company, he was called upon to work. It was his job and nobody criticized him for it.

Baseball was *my* job. It was how I made my living, supported my family, and found a way to witness for Christ. Besides that, I made it a rule always to attend church first. I've never yet run into a manager who complained when an over-long sermon made me report late to the ball park.

Another question sure to be asked was how my teammates reacted to my Christian convictions. I believe my answer is true in baseball or anywhere else in life. Any man will command respect if he takes a stand and backs it up with his life. If the life doesn't reflect the testimony, however, the result is contempt.

In my first attempts to speak in public, I was nervous and afraid of saying the wrong thing. Betsy helped me to overcome that. She urged me simply to say what was in my heart and leave the results with God.

My trouble that winter, and for several winters to come, was my inability to say "no." Every invitation to speak seemed a valuable opportunity to present my testimony—and a refusal to speak, a turning away from my duty as a Christian. Hadn't God put me into baseball to witness for Him?

Betsy and the children suffered from my absences, and I was to learn much later, after the speaking engagements pushed me to the point of exhaustion, that a man's first responsibility before God is to his immediate family.

I took Betsy and Robby to spring training with me in 1958 and it was a tough experience for all of us. Day after day of rain washed out the practice sessions and kept us holed up in a tiny bedroom-and-kitchenette apartment six blocks from the ball park. Robby was sick with a bad cold nearly the whole time, and while on the field I fought an uncertain battle for the shortstop position and lost.

When we went north, McDougald was stationed at second, Tony Kubek at short, and Andy Carey at third. I was the utility man destined for little utility. I'd considered my participation in 97 games during 1957 pretty bad. I was to feel worse about the 73 games in which I would see action that next year.

At one time or another, every player has trouble trying to get out of a slump. I didn't have that trouble—I stayed in the slump all year.

Casey used to look at me and say, "Look at him. He doesn't drink, doesn't smoke, and he still can't hit .250!"

"To hit, you have to play," I kept telling him. But it was uncomfortable knowing an image of me was forming, an image of a player who simply couldn't hit major league ball. A number of fine rookies have started out with a slump, been pegged as good-field-no-hit, and sent down, never to be seen again. Once you're a veteran, it's different. You can bat 0-for-20 and no one is seriously troubled.

Riding the bench is tough all by itself. But during road trips, it's worse. There's so much glamour associated with professional baseball that few people realize the temptations a player faces when he's away from his family so much.

Unclean conversation provides the climate in which temptation flourishes. Gambling, drinking, and promiscuity are made easy when the location is a plush hotel far from home. This is no indictment against any particular player, team, or league. It's just a straight look at the facts.

The 1958 season rolled on slowly and my uneasiness on the bench grew. It didn't help when Ronnie was born July 13 during the first game of a long double-header at Yankee Stadium. I'd taken Betsy to the hospital at 5 that morning and at 2 P.M. Dr. John Glasser called the stadium with the news that I was the father of another son. I kept warming the bench as the second game droned on past the hospital's visiting hours. I wasn't able to see Betsy and my new son until the next day.

In spite of what was, in many ways, my toughest season, there was one light moment I'll never forget. It happened when the Yanks traveled to Detroit after clinching the pennant in Kansas City the day before. The general management had decided to keep a sharp eye out for its players lest high living incapacitate them for the important contest a week or so away. But when word slipped out that a battery of private detectives had been hired to "tail" members of the team, things went from the sublime to the ridiculous.

The "private eyes" evidently hadn't boned up on the living habits of John Kucks and Bobby Shantz, not to mention Kubek and I who were dubbed "The Milk-shake Twins." When the four of us left the hotel early one evening, we became aware that we were being shad-owed. Actually we were on our way to the YMCA several blocks distant where we were going to settle, once and for all, who was the best ping-pong player on the team. We ducked into doorways, faked our way in and out of a theater, and kept the detectives huffing and puffing after us for quite some time before we arrived at the Y.

The investigators were gone when we emerged some time later. I don't know whether their top secret report carried the results of our game, but Johnny Kucks beat me out for the ping-pong championship.

I was thrilled in Milwaukee when Casey started me in one of the games against the National League champs. But disappointment followed when I went 0-for-5 against Warren Spahn and was pulled out for the rest of the Series.

Quitting baseball had been on my mind during the latter part of that season. Benched and inactive, I felt that my life was of little use to the Lord. How much better to return to Sumter, go to college, and prepare for fulltime Christian service?

Ralph Houk, now general manager of the New York Yankees, talked me out of it. Through professional baseball, he said, I could contact thousands of youngsters and witness to my faith. In his thinking, the opportunities for service were greater in Yankee Stadium than in a pulpit or a church camp. After thinking it over and praying about it, I agreed.

As a substitute plan, after I returned home that fall I

enrolled at Columbia Bible College about 45 miles to the east of Sumter. But even that didn't work out. My father had been ailing for several months. Now X rays proved that he had contracted tuberculosis. He was admitted to a sanitarium in Florence, an 85-mile drive from Columbia, and I had no alternative but to withdraw from school. There was no one to take mother to visit him and for a while that winter his condition had everyone concerned. As it turned out, he stayed in the sanitarium six months and returned home much improved.

With school out of the question, I turned my attention toward radio and took over a 15-minute sports program aired 3 times a week over Sumter Station WFIG. That activity, which I continued for three years, afforded much satisfaction. It was made up of taped interviews with major league players which I recorded during the baseball season, plus late news as it came in over the ticker tape. Each program concluded with an interview with a local youth.

That winter I received a long distance phone call from Jerry Coleman. He'd been offered the job of assistant to the Yankee farm manager, and as part of his new duties he wanted to know if I'd be returning the next spring. I told him of my talk with Houk and my decision to stick with the club in the hope that I'd be able to play regularly in the upcoming season.

I received a generous $3,000 boost in pay that brought my annual salary to $11,000, but when spring training was over in 1959, it looked like another year on the bench for me.

MacDougald started at second, Kubek at short, and Carey at third. I began to envy two of my friends, Norm Siebern and Jerry Lumpe who were Yankee bench-warmers in 1958 but who were traded early in 1959. Both were now playing every day even though they weren't playing for the Yankees.

One day, three weeks after the regular season had started, I walked into the office of Assistant General Manager Roy Hamey and asked to be traded. He was sympathetic but said the Yankees planned no further trades of younger players.

"Be patient," he told me, "you'll get your chance."

I departed the office unconvinced, but within a week McDougald was injured and I was installed at second. When Gil returned to action, he went to third. I stayed on for the season at the keystone spot.

Casey was still suspicious of my hitting ability and batted me eighth. When Larsen or Byrne were pitching (both were good stickmen) I batted ninth behind them.

Whenever the game was critical—and sometimes when it wasn't—I'd be pulled out for a pinch-hitter.

That was a wonderful way to keep me humble but one day I cracked. It was the first inning of a game in Cleveland. We had taken a 3-0 lead and had 3 men on base. As I went to the plate, I heard Casey's familiar yell, "Hold that gun!"

Enos Slaughter was sent to the plate instead. In a display of temper, I threw my helmet down and went into the showers. Before I could turn on the water, Casey appeared.

"Get into uniform. We need a bullpen catcher."

Dressing again, I had time to cool off. Casey was right. He usually was. He wanted to get a strong first-inning lead, and with the bases loaded he needed a proven power hitter.

I found out afterwards that Enos, whose lifetime average was over .300, hit into a double play.

Then Bill Dickey, our batting coach, began to give me some extra attention. The all-time great Yankee catcher and hitter had a simple rule: swing with authority. He knew I was no power hitter but he didn't tell me what I'd heard so often: get a lighter bat and choke up. Instead he advised a heavier bat and urged me to swing with everything I had!

He knew I didn't miss the ball often but he reasoned that soft-hit balls can't make it through the infield.

"Lazy balls get caught," he said.

I followed his unorthodox advice and began to poke more and more base hits through the holes at short and second. When the last game of the 1959 season rolled around, I was batting .298.

We were in Baltimore and Billy O'Dell was the Orioles' pitcher that day. To my surprise, Casey came up to me before the start of the game and said, "Get a couple hits and I'll take you out of the lineup."

I knew the Yanks were out of pennant contention and the game was not crucial, but I was surprised that Stengel had been following my average.

I was further surprised when Brooks Robinson, the Bird's All-Star third baseman, came over and practically invited me to bunt.

"I'll be playing deep today," he said, laughing.

A few moments later Ed Hurley, the first-base umpire, called me over.

"Just make it close," he told me.

With all this going for me, I half expected the catcher to give me the sign of what O'Dell was throwing. But I knew Billy, a good friend and hunting partner, was wishing me well.

As it turned out, I hit a line drive right into Albie Pierson's glove in right field my first time up. Next I got a base hit with a looping single to short center field. The third time, I hit a grounder up the middle that rolled into center field.

Stengel phoned the club statistician who did some quick figuring and reported that my average had climbed to .301. I was immediately taken out of the game and a pinch-runner sent to take my place on first. As I left the field, I could almost hear the Baltimore dugout cheering for me.

12

World Series Thrills

THAT WINTER I accepted the chairmanship of the state tuberculosis campaign and again found my calendar crowded with speaking engagements. I was also approached by the American Tract Society to put my testimony into print, and when it was distributed throughout the country I began to be deluged with speaking invitations. I saw that it was utterly impossible to accept anything but a small share of them, but I kept doggedly at it, still nagged by a sense of guilt whenever I had to sit down and write a letter of refusal.

In the 1960 season my batting average fell to .252. I hit one homer in April and noted that the pitcher who permitted it was sent back to the minors the next day.

I was pressing too hard for the base hits. I drove the ball well when I connected but somebody always seemed to be there to catch it. In 460 times at bat in 150 games, I collected only 26 RBI's.

I fear I gave Betsy little support that year in the challenging task of being a baseball player's wife. She had to make a home for me and the children in 3 different

locations every year—Sumter, St. Petersburg, and Ridgewood (N.J.), where we rented a house during the season. Because I was on the road half the time, she had to
be part-time plumber, mechanic, and chauffeur, as well
as a diaper-changer, housekeeper, secretary, and my
Number-One Fan.

Her conviction that God had called me into baseball
helped her over the rough spots and she worked hard
to provide an atmosphere at home in which I could
relax from baseball.

Absorbed as I was in my batting problems, I sometimes got into trouble in other areas. Early in 1960 I'd
been given the honor of being player representative for
the team. As part of my responsibilities, I called the
meeting toward the end of the season for the taking of
the official team picture. It was a command performance, unlike press and publicity photos. Everybody was
expected to be on the dot, suited up and ready. The
picture was a color shot, the one used in yearbooks and
sports history books, and especially important that year
because it was the twenty-fifth anniversary of the Yankee organization.

I notified all the players to be at the park on the
appointed day and then occupied myself with other
matters. The night before the all-important date, my
brother-in-law, Heyward Strong, flew in from Florida
and we had a good visit, sitting up late, talking and
reminiscing. Early the next morning I took him to the

airport. It was hours before game time so I decided to drive back to our home in Ridgewood and come in later with Spud Murray, our batting practice pitcher, who lived nearby. I called Spud and found he'd already left. Funny, he'd be coming in so early, I mused. But dismissing the thought, I decided to take it easy, go back home anyway, play with the kids, loaf around a bit.

About 11 A.M., I left home again in a relaxed mood and began my leisurely drive into the stadium— when it hit me! Glancing at my watch I saw that I was already 15 minutes past the deadline I'd set for all the players to be in uniform and on the field for the picture. I didn't know whether to stop the car and crawl into a manhole in the street, go back home and go to bed, or just keep on driving. I chose the latter and when I reached the ball park, the picture had already been taken. I really got the raspberry from my teammates and a few well-chosen words from Mr. Stengel.

During the World Series that year, many people were asking, "Who is this Bobby Richardson?"—unable to spot anybody by that name on the big official photo that emblazoned the series program. I had to tell the whole embarrassing story over again to the sports writers.

That was a year when prayer brought new peace to both Betsy and me. For some time she had been disturbed by my absences from our growing family caused by speaking engagements during the off-season and the long road trips during the season. The road trips made me edgy too. I didn't like the seemingly endless travel and spending so much time in towns far from home.

One day Betsy poured out all her concern before the Lord. And the answer came. She was not to be troubled by the special circumstances that surrounded my vocation. If they were part of my calling, she was to accept the limitations and find in God the peace to live with them.

The Lord answered her prayer in another way, too. I began using the time on the long road trips for serious Bible study. The more earnestly I pursued it, the more satisfaction and peace resulted.

That year the Yanks won the pennant and went into the World Series against the Pittsburgh Pirates. In the third game, I had the thrill of my career.

We were in the lead 3-0 in the first inning when I came to bat with the bases loaded. As I walked to the plate, my ears were tuned to hear the familiar, "Hold that gun!" and to step aside for a pinch hitter. But the dugout was quiet, and glancing at third-base coach Frank Crosetti, I saw the sign was on for a bunt.

I took a deep breath, waited, and tried to bunt the pitch, fouling it off instead. Strike one. Another glance at Crosetti and this time he had me hitting. I was hoping for a hit to right in order to stay clear of a double play. When the pitch came I swung and instead saw it head into left. As I rounded first I feared Gino Cimoli had caught the ball. But he'd stopped at the fence. The ball went into the stands behind him. However the full realization of what had happened didn't sweep over me until I crossed home plate and Howard, Skowron, and McDougald, the men on base, were pounding me on the back and shouting over the roar of the crowd.

As the game progressed, I came to bat again with the bases loaded and couldn't help but think of how nice it would be if I could tap one more out of the park. But I was grateful to settle for a line drive single scoring two runs and setting a record for the largest number of RBI's in a single World Series game.

As I looked back over the season, I was amazed at the record and the 12 RBI's, record best for a seven-game series. Certainly it wouldn't have happened if time and again I didn't come to bat with men on base. This illustrates how circumstances can help or hinder the performance at the plate.

Records are made to be broken and these two are sure to be shattered as the years pass. Only one mark is certain to stand, in my estimation, and that is Joe DiMaggio's record of hitting in 56 consecutive games. I can't believe that streak will ever be topped.

The Yanks lost the '60 Series with the famous seventh-game, ninth-inning homer by Bill Mazeroski, but for me it had been a Series I'll never forget.

Still more surprises were in store for me. Driving back to Sumter with Betsy and the kids in the brand new Corvette I'd been awarded by *Sport* magazine, we were stopped about 20 miles from home by a highway patrol roadblock. From there on into town, we were given a police escort, and when we arrived 10,000 people were on hand to welcome us home.

They had me make a speech at the courthouse, then proclaimed me honorary mayor, good-will ambassador, and honorary chief of police. A big parade followed.

I can't believe any town on earth could have been more generous to us through the years. In 1959, during halftime in the high school's annual Homecoming Football Game, we'd been given a washing machine and dryer, furniture, a case of shotgun shells, and fire trucks for the boys. The year before that, at an Appreciation Night banquet, I'd been presented a 16-gauge, 5-shot automatic Browning shotgun.

Red Kneece, president of the Sumter YMCA board, had called me toward the end of the season and asked me to take over as general secretary on an interim basis during the off-season. And I'd agreed to do it.

I had a real love for the Y. I had learned to swim there as a boy and had played in almost every athletic program they sponsored. I'd seen the fine job the Sumter Y had done over the years in the lives of countless youngsters.

I soon found that being general secretary was a fulltime job. The facilities in Sumter were run down and there was no fulltime physical education director. There was good help otherwise and fine public support, so with the board's approval, a permanent general secretary was acquired and a drive was launched for a new building.

Bob Vetter, a graduate of Columbia Bible College and an experienced YMCA leader in New York City, came to Sumter and took over as general secretary. The program has grown stronger every year since and in 1964 the building drive went over the top.

That was probably my hardest working off-season, made more difficult by my decision to build a house. All that winter, when the home was under construction, Betsy tried to convey our wishes to the contractor while she doubled as mom and dad to the boys, and in December gave birth to Christie, our first girl. We left for spring training on March 1, the day our new home was finished.

Casey Stengel had been released when we lost the Series the previous fall, and our new manager was Ralph Houk. I hated to see Casey leave. He'd been more than fair to me through the years, giving me valuable advice and providing many opportunities to play when he really didn't have to.

On the other hand I was pleased to see Ralph move up. He'd been with the Yankee organization twenty-two years and had piled up a tremendous record. Although he'd played in only ninety-one major league games, the reason was simple: he was playing behind Yogi Berra. Switched to staff, he coached in 1953 and 1954, then became manager at Denver for three highly successful years, '55, '56, and '57. I knew from my two years at Denver that he was a tremendous manager and in New

York would be a worthy successor to Miller Huggins, Joe McCarthy, and Casey.

Ralph moved me from eighth to second place in the batting order, a gesture I really appreciated. For two years at Denver under Houk I'd batted second; and sometimes, against lefthanded pitchers, I'd batted third. Nothing pleased me more. At this spot I had a chance to hit-and-run, start the base runner on his way, then poke the ball through the hole at short or second. This spot on the batting order also provided ample opportunity to bunt, another activity I enjoyed.

It was an easy season and the Yanks put away the pennant early, due largely to the tremendous hitting of Roger Maris and Mickey Mantle. I led the team in hits, 173, and collected 49 RBI's, but that record couldn't hold a candle to Roger's mark of 61 homeruns and 142 RBI's. Mantle rapped out 54 homers and picked up 128 RBI's.

That was the year when Roger's achievement in breaking Babe Ruth's record of 60 homeruns in a season earned for the slugging right-fielder the coveted Hickok belt marking him as the top professional athlete of the year. Among other awards, he repeated as the American League's Most Valuable Player.

I remember the pressure Roger was under in the closing games of the 1961 season. Reporters hounded him everywhere and fired the same question again and again, "Do you think you're going to surpass Ruth's record?"

On one occasion, when Maris had homered in a game,

the reporters poured into the locker room looking for him and completely bypassed Elston Howard's locker. Ellie had hit a 3-run homer in the same game but hardly anybody noticed.

I played in every contest that season and sometimes, with the pennant pressure off, it was hard to keep alert hour after hour through the long doubleheaders. Occasionally I'd pretend to be announcing the game over the radio. I did that once in a game at Chicago with nearly disastrous results.

"And now, here comes Pete Ward," I said to myself. "Ball one, a curve ball. . . . Ball two, fast ball. . . . Here's the next one. Ward swings and there's a grounder to sec—ulp, *that's me!*" I came to life in time to stop the ball but not cleanly. It bounced off my chest and was called a hit but I knew it should have been an error.

I like radio announcing and if the Lord leads in that direction I may do more of it some day. I like sports announcing especially because there's an opportunity to be free and easy, spontaneous, and conversational. I know I'll have a tough time with the commercials, though—so many of them have to be read or memorized.

One of the relatively few times I agreed to do a television commercial, I nearly put the film director into a fit. I've never permitted my name to be associated with liquor or cigarettes or anything else I thought might be harmful to youth. Razor blades seemed a pretty safe bet but it took the TV crew 9 takes to get me to do everything right. My line was supposed to be, "Smooth! You can hardly tell there's a blade in the razor!" But when I got through squirting shaving cream all over everybody, I'd invariably say, "Smooth! You can hardly tell there's a rade in the blazer!"

Eventually the long 1961 season drew to a close and once again we entered the World Series, this time against the determined Cincinnati Reds. Mickey was playing after recent surgery on his hip and ought to have been in a hospital room instead of at the field. But his one big blow was a key hit that year and I believe it provided the inspiration that carried us through to victory. John Blanchard's .400 hitting and 2 homers were tremendous contributions, too.

During the series I picked up 9 hits but no RBI's—further evidence, if anybody needs it, that a big RBI total is related to a circumstance over which you have no control and can't be given credit for: the number of men on base when you come up to bat.

13

New Friends

DURING THE WINTER of 1961-62 Paul Alderman, a prominent Sumter layman, approached me with the idea of collecting a team of Christian athletes and presenting testimonies for Christ in every South Carolina high school which would accept us. After praying it over, I too became convinced that God was calling for such a move.

The previous year, through the Fellowship of Christian Athletes, I'd met a number of professional sportsmen who had given their lives to the Lord. At citywide meetings in Columbia, I'd been invited to speak with Frank Broyles, head football coach at Arkansas, Clendon Thomas, a professional football player and All-American from Okahoma University, and big Bill Glass, defensive end of the Cleveland Browns.

An experience Bill and I had that week gave me an added reason to be enthusiastic about high-school meetings. Bill and I secured permission to give our testimonies at the state penitentiary in Columbia and I'll never forget standing up before those men and telling them of the gospel.

One boy among the prisoners asked us a question which has haunted me ever since: "Why is it that I hear of Jesus Christ *here* and for the first time in my life?"

Who could answer his question? I know that most states in our country have laws requiring a Bible to be placed in every cell of every penitentiary; yet in these same states and elsewhere, the use of the Bible in the public schools is under sharp attack. Teachers are forbidden to read it to their students or teach obedience to it as God's Word.

Something seems terribly wrong.

I got busy on the phone that February in 1962 while Paul started lining up the schools we might visit. Before long 4 other athletes agreed to join me for the mission: Jerry Kindall, then second baseman for the Cleveland Indians; Johnny Spence, a PGA golf pro at Columbia; Mel Peterson, former Little All-American of the Wheaton College basketball team, and Raymond Berry, Baltimore Colts end.

It was a thrilling experience. May it be said to the credit of South Carolina that only one high school refused us. Most gave us a tremendous welcome and an attentive hearing. Many boys and girls made confessions of faith in Jesus Christ.

Although Bill Glass had been unable to attend these meetings, my friendship with him deepened after the experience at the penitentiary. Some of our experiences have even had comic overtones.

During the winter Bill and Don Shinnick, linebacker of the Baltimore Colts, and I were invited to speak before 10,000 young people gathered in Washington, D.C., for a giant weekend Youth for Christ rally.

One of the nights we had to wear tuxedos to a banquet honoring ambassadors of many countries. Dave Swanson, director of the Long Island Youth for Christ and a close friend, had rented tuxedos for Bill and me, and 15 minutes before we were to leave for the banquet, I dashed up to my hotel room to change.

Imagine my consternation when I pulled on the pants and found the legs about *a foot too long!* Betsy wanted me to take them back but there was no time for that, so I pulled the suspenders tight, hoisted the beltline to my armpits, and hoped the coat would cover it up. With pants still too long, I laboriously pinned the cuffs under. With the clock running out, I finally slipped on the coat—and got another shock. I looked like a circus clown, the shoulders six inches too wide and the sleeves completely hiding my hands.

I was frantic, and then there was a knock at the door. Bill stepped in, still dressed in street clothes.

"How's your tux?" I asked him.

"Terrible," he said, "I can't get into it!"

Then the truth dawned. A moment later I gave my tux to 6-foot, 5-inch, 265-pound Bill Glass and he gave me the tux he'd been struggling with. All was well for the big appearance.

As each year passed, my mail had grown heavier. I was making more friends across the country and correspondence with them was increasing. But other types of mail were coming my way too and I was jolted by them.

I got my first taste of a new kind of mail when I began to go in at second base for Billy Martin. Following his trade to Kansas City, I caught the written reaction of some of his fans.

"What kind of a guy are you, anyway? How can you treat Billy that way?"—etc., etc., etc.

I was stymied. How could I explain that managers, not players, make position changes?

Then other letters came, many from small churches, some from individuals, relating stories of suffering and struggle and asking for money. Letters came from people professing to know Christ, some asking quite earnestly about how I could play Sunday ball as a Christian; some others were full of condemnation. Sometimes I'd get a series of letters about Sunday ball, criticizing me roundly and using Billy Sunday, a baseball player who quit to become an evangelist, as evidence that I was out of the will of God. (My own point of view is given at the beginning of Chapter 11.)

After one World Series in which I committed a costly error, a man wrote requesting 25 dollars. He'd bet that much that the Yanks would win, and when they lost he felt I should refund the money inasmuch as my error had contributed to the defeat.

Other letters arrived from young sports-minded Christians seeking all kinds of advice. One boy was troubled about a batting slump. He'd tried not to swing until he had 2 strikes. He'd tried swinging at the first pitch, crowding the plate, getting deep in the batter's box, just about everything. Would I, in a letter, give him the answer to his problem?

Other letters probed deeper. "When did you know that basebell was your calling?" "Do you pray for a good day or that your team will win?" "Do you feel that slumps and errors are sometimes sent by God to test your faith?"

A valuable contribution to the Keep-Bobby-Humble department were letters from fans asking me to secure Mickey Mantle's autograph for them.

It came over me gradually that some people identify so closely with professional athletes that they feel a sense of ownership. Once, during a game at Washington, my throw to Tony at second was in the dirt, good enough for a putout but not good enough to make the double play. After the game, when it turned out that my throw had been fatal to our cause, I was approached by Casey in the clubhouse.

"Somebody wants you on the phone," he said.

It was a long distance call, loaded with profanity, demanding that I repay the caller for money he'd lost betting on the Yankees.

Phone calls began to be a major problem as people contacted me to participate in such diverse activities as ground-breaking ceremonies, ship christenings, church fund-raising bazaars, overseas coaching clinics, and beauty contests. (I have yet to figure out how being a second baseman for the Yankees qualifies me as a judge of a beauty contest!)

Around World Series time, requests poured in for tickets, some with money enclosed, many with I'll-pay-you-later postscripts added. In later years I averaged an out-of-pocket loss of from $500 to $1000 annually due to unpaid-for tickets. I'm sure most of the people thought players were given an unlimited number of free tickets; others simply forgot to reimburse me.

As a matter of fact, only a few free tickets are allotted players in each game played—with World Series tickets not included.

Another fact largely unknown by fans is the American League rule that any player in uniform is forbidden to respond to calls from the sidelines or stands. Each time he ignores the rule, he is fined. Many friends across the country have come down to the screen before game time and shouted, "Hey Bobby!"

If I can ignore the call without hurting their feelings, I do. If not, I come over to say hello. I'm not trying to be unfriendly. It's just that each chat costs me 10 dollars.

A separate chapter could be written about autograph hunters. They are everywhere—inside the ball park,

Top: A slide into first sometimes rattles the defensive player. Joe Adcock was pulled off the base in a game at the Stadium in 1963. (PHOTOGRAPH BY THE NEW YORK TIMES.)

Right: Sometimes it gets pretty rough behind second base. (PHOTOGRAPH BY THE NEW YORK TIMES.)

Bottom: Several years I've helped out in a baseball clinic at the Sumter YMCA. The "Y" is an organization I stand behind wholeheartedly.

I wouldn't even try to make a baseball player of this little lady—my older daughter, Chris

waiting at the dressing room door, outside on the sidewalk when the players emerge to call a cab, at the hotel lobby, in the hotel dining room, and sometimes in the upstairs hallways, pacing back and forth, hoping to run into a player. When the men finally get back to their hotel rooms and relax, the phones begin to ring. Autograph collectors in the lobby are asking if they can come up or when the players plan to come down.

Here, too, the Keep-Bobby-Humble department has been strengthened. More than once, when I've been in a hotel lobby with other members of the team, a youngster has approached me and asked, "Are you a player for the Yankees?"

"Yes."

"Would you please ask Mickey Mantle over there to sign this baseball?"

Mickey, of course, is mobbed wherever he goes. Understandably, he has his hotel phone disconnected or rigged so that only certain calls are permitted to go through. Sometimes he has to take refuge in another hotel. If he didn't, he'd never have a moment of peace.

Actually, most autograph hunters are youngsters and they're a swell bunch. They are loyal fans and its flattering that they put such value on a signature. Frankly, I enjoy talking with them when there is time, and when things are rushed they always seem to understand.

Their mothers are a different matter.

Many a player has been publicly humiliated by an irate mother who simply cannot understand how he could be so "cruel" as not to sign an autograph book.

"There you are a, big-shot ball player, making money hand over fist, and you can't take 2 seconds out to scribble your name for my son!"

Sometimes I'm a little ashamed about the attention and acclaim that so often surrounds the professional athlete. Isn't it inconsistent with the lowly character of Christian discipleship? Isn't the constant praise of men a temptation to become proud?

I can only offer the answer I gave in the American Tract Society leaflet:

> We must have a purpose in life, and that purpose should be to please God—to know Him, to love Him, to walk with Him in our daily lives.
>
> Baseball is a profession full of temptations, just as are other professions, and it is a challenge to lead a Christian life in the midst of it. But I take my stand on a Bible verse that has strengthened and challenged me because I know to claim it means a completely surrendered life.
>
> *"I am crucified with Christ; nevertheless I live, yet not I, but Christ liveth in me; and the life which I live in the flesh I live by the faith of the Son of God, who loved me, and gave himself for me"* (Galatians 2:20).

I realize simply that it is God who has given me the ability, the opportunity and certainly any supposed earthly glory that might come through playing ball. I enjoy the sport I am in, but only because I feel that this is where God would have me serve Him.

14

Practical Jokes

THE YEAR 1962 was my most productive one for the Yankees. I played in every game but one and batted .302 with 8 homers, my all-time high. This must be attributed largely to Ralph Houk who had confidence in me and kept me in there even when my batting wasn't as sharp as it could have been. He stayed with me through the slumps, didn't pull me out for pinch hitters, and it gave me a great desire to reward his confidence with a good performance.

I had a good year but I'm afraid it wasn't as good as many people in Sumter thought. The reason was John Quackenbush, a local sportscaster, who used to recreate the Yankee games over Sumter Station WFIG. Because the regular network broadcast of our games was too far away for most receivers and was protected by copyright against rebroadcast, John became an expert at *simulating* the game. Sitting in his studio in a Sumter storefront, he'd get a continuous wire-service ticker tape of the contest about an inning or two later than the action, and sportscast the game to Sumter listeners *as though he were watching it live in New York.* He'd add a few remarks from time to time that would boost that impression.

"Well, Mel [Mel Allen, the Yankee sportscaster, reported on games from the pressbox high over the stadium in New York] it looks like we've got a close one today.

"I see the flags are blowing briskly to the right. That means a good day for the lefthanded hitters.

"There's Sumter's own Robert Richardson coming into the dugout. Just looked up and gave me a wave. Good luck, Bobby!"

In that sort of broadcast, John had ample opportunity to embellish my accomplishments a bit because he knew many of my friends and well-wishers were listening.

He'd snap his pencil against the console in the control room, a sound impossible to distinguish from the distant sound of a bat hitting a ball, and he'd shout, "There's a slashing line drive off the bat of Bobby Richardson!" At the same time he'd turn up a sound-effects record of a roaring, cheering crowd. Then he'd add, "Brooks Robinson goes after it! He's got it! A terrific diving catch!"

I'm afraid many Sumterites got the impression over the years that every ball I hit was a slashing line drive or a towering sky-high belt into deep center field (but inside the fence), and that opposition players had to pull off miracle plays to stop me.

That was the year when I began to see myself in the faces of the younger players coming up. Now I was in

the spot Billy Martin was in back in 1958. *I* was the
veteran who had somehow weathered the storms and
become a fixture in the lineup. Eager, ambitious, hard-
working rookies sat on the bench every day, and I knew
what they were thinking—*"Just give me a chance."*

I could tell it in the hustle and determination they
showed in the pregame warmups. They wanted somebody's job.

I tried to steer them over to short while Tony tried to
impress them with the great possibilities at second base.
Joe Pepitone was satisfied as long as they ignored first
base.

There was the usual amount of kidding, but actually
it was no cinch to break into the lineup that year. This
was the competition:

Clete Boyer—in my opinion, the best defensive third
baseman in the game, with an instinct for making the
great plays, diving for the ball, and firing to first from a
fallen-down position.

Tony Kubek—made all the plays at the shortstop position. Best throw out of the deep hole I've ever seen.
Proved outfielder via Casey's platooning and my best
friend and roommate.

Joe Pepitone—coming up as an outfielder, Joe broke
into the first base spot where he was now firmly established. He had a good performance record behind him
and was still improving.

Elston Howard—for many years a backup catcher for
Yogi; often overlooked was his record of consistent
power-hitting. Had one of the best arms in baseball.

Pitchers had confidence in him because he called a good game.

Tommy Tresh—only leftfielder since Gene Woodling who could make the play in left field that limits the batter to a single. Hit with power from both sides of the plate and was able to play all the outfield positions plus shortstop.

Roger Maris—hard-playing power hitter and an excellent runner. Could go back on the ball as well as anyone, had a strong arm, and was an expert at breaking up the double play.

Mickey Mantle—in spite of repeated injuries, Mickey could do more to win games than anybody else I knew. He was a switch hitter and could bunt, steal a base, and go from first to third as fast as any player in either league. Underrated was his large number of bases-on-balls. In addition to all this, his leadership ability on the team was invaluable.

Whitey Ford—an all-time pitching great with an excellent attitude toward the game. Never got rattled, bore down when men got on base, and never seemed upset when infielders' errors put him in trouble.

Jim Bouton and Al Downing—top-flight hurlers with attitudes to match Whitey's, made up part of a formidable pitching staff.

This didn't discourage the rookies, however. They worked hard, practiced long, and sat through the games on the bench, watching and learning. They weren't discouraged, either, by the practical joking that singles out rookies for special attention.

Practical Jokes

Once Jake Gibbs was phoned up by Tony Kubek, posing as a sportswriter. Elston had come down with food poisoning, the "writer" said, and the manager had told the press that Jake would start as catcher the next day.

"That's all right with me!" Jake said, thrilled by the unexpected opportunity to prove himself.

"You mean, it's all right with you that Howard is sick?"

"Oh, no! No, I don't mean that! I mean I'm just glad to play!"

"Would you describe for our readers just how you feel on this important night of your career?"

On and on it went until Jake began to wonder what all the snickering was about on the other end of the line.

Another trick played year after year is the note stuck in the locker directing the rookie to phone a "Mr. Lyon." When he dials the number and asks for "Mr. Lyon," he usually gets a sarcastic reply from the office of the Bronx Park Zoo.

One youngster who was especially trusting was Mike Mathiason. Time and again one of the players would call him up on the bullpen phone and say that Houk wanted him in the game right away. He'd go running up to Ralph, full of ginger and ready to go, only to find it was a false alarm.

One day when Houk *really did* want Mike, the rookie was in the clubhouse, and I was out of breath when I found him. "Mike! Houk wants you to fill in at third right away! Boyer's been injured!"

He looked at me in disgust. "I know. I know. He's dying to put me in."

It suddenly came over me that we'd kidded him once too often. "I'm not foolin' this time, Mike! Houk really does want you in!"

"Go tell him I don't want to play now. Maybe later. I'll see how I feel."

I started laughing and he took it as additional evidence that the whole thing was a joke. He refused to take me seriously and I departed, my mission a failure.

Fortunately Ralph was the type to understand when I explained, and another player was put in at third. Sometime later Mike appeared, learned what had happened, and walked around stunned for the rest of the day.

Of course, rookies aren't the only ones victimized by practical jokes. John Blanchard, no newcomer to the Yank roster, was dozing in the whirlpool machine one day, easing a sore muscle, when Mantle poured into the water a whole bottle of shampoo. Johnny nearly disappeared in the mountain of suds that came up from nowhere.

On another occasion Blanchard tired of an old straw hat he had in his locker and threw it into a trash can. The action was observed by Pete Sheehy, a Yankee organization man for twenty-five years and boss of the clubhouse. He slyly recovered the hat from the trash sometime later and put it back in John's locker.

The husky catcher did a double-take when he came across the hat the next time, but in disgust threw it away again. By that time Pete had engaged the willing services of two or three players and each time John discarded the hat it was duly recovered and returned. Even when the team was on the road, this happened. Discarded in Detroit, the hat, now looking more ragged than ever, would show up in Los Angeles. The last time we saw the hat was one day in the New York clubhouse when John, in desperation, set fire to it. With a feeling of sadness, the rest of us stood around and watched it burn.

Baseball men are unmerciful joke players. Show distaste for something—spinach, long distance calls, purple ties, anything—and you're in for it.

Phil Rizzuto had no special affection for bugs, worms, caterpillars, etc. As a result, when he went up to bat all sorts of interesting things were stuffed into the fingers of his glove, to be discovered when he ran out to field later.

Marshall Bridges, a Yankee pitcher who shared Phil's distaste for creeping things, was the butt of similar jokes. Once a rubber snake, refrigerated just enough to make it cold and slippery, was placed in the pants leg of Marshall's baseball uniform. There was an air of pleasant expectancy in the locker room when he slipped one leg into the pants, then the other, then withdrew one leg, reached down and came up with the snake. You could have heard his reaction at the other end of the stadium.

On another occasion, Marshall was drawn into a conversation about hunting which had been rigged in advance. Mickey had purchased a pistol and loaded it with blanks. He gestured with it as he told a story about a man who shot somebody with a gun thought to be unloaded.

"It was like this one," Mantle illustrated, pointing the gun at Marshall, "this one isn't loaded, either"—and pulled the trigger! There was a loud report!

"Oh! I'm shot!" Bridges exclaimed, clutching his chest and staggering back.

Sometimes the jokes don't turn out to be as funny as intended. On April Fool's Day in 1964, several of us urged Yogi to tell Steve Hamilton he'd just been traded to Washington. Straight-faced, Yogi approached the lanky pitcher who was working out during a pregame warmup.

"Steve, I hate to say this but we've just sent you back to the Senators. I tried to stop it but the front office went over my head."

Steve looked stricken. He'd been traded several times and had recently arrived from the Senators. His eyes filled with tears. Fortunately, Whitey Ford came running up, shouting, "April Fool!"

Sometimes the tricks go on during the game between members of the opposing teams.

At an exhibition game during spring training in 1957, we were playing against the Phillies in New Orleans. Most of the first-string players were excused after the fifth inning and the rookies took over. I belted a triple and came sliding into third base, proud and happy, hoping the management had noticed the play. Veteran Phillies third-sacker Puddin' Head Jones, a native South Carolinian like myself, looked at me unimpressed. He seemed insulted that I'd dirtied his base bag.

"How about kicking that bag, get the dirt off it?" he said.

Obligingly I stepped off, hauled back to kick and was promptly tagged by Jones who had hidden the ball in his glove.

The umpire didn't see the maneuver, so in spite of Puddin' Head's loud objection I was permitted to stay on base.

"How can one South Carolinian do something like that to another?" I muttered. But it was simple. On and off the field, you have to keep alert in baseball.

I enjoy the lighthearted side of the sport, but I'm essentially serious. And during these years, the important things have been happening inside me. My walk with the Lord has been getting simpler, more direct, and my prayer life more intimate.

For many years I'd prayed chiefly at night. Now, each morning, I began to place the day in the Lord's hands.

There were other opportunities too—before meals and when under particular temptation. Every game we played started with the national anthem. I began to use that hushed moment as a time to ask that God be glorified in anything I might do during the game.

A special time each night I'm home is bedtime for Robby, Ronnie, Christie, and Jeannie (the last-named joined the family circle in early 1964). I read a child's devotional book or a Bible story, then lead a discussion. Finally we pray together, following the lines of what we've learned.

By itself, of course, prayer has no value. The example of a Christ-filled life must go along with it. Children, simple as they are, understand this.

The story is told of a father who carefully described to his son what a Christian was—truthful, loving, patient, gentle. When he finished, the boy had a question. "Daddy, have I ever seen a Christian?"

The power of prayer and a Christian life were brought home to me dramatically a few years earlier when I'd first been told of Brookland Plantation, a work inspired by the Rev. Ralph Wentling. Brookland is an old southern mansion near Sumter where two dedicated Christian men, Director "Pop" Lambert and Bob Potter, live with about twenty boys, some of whom have been given up by the courts as incorrigible. At the mansion the boys live under strict discipline; they are loved and given the gospel.

I was deeply impressed by the transformed lives of the youngsters there, and I joined the board of directors, giving as much time and service as I've been able to.

Prayer is a privilege and I've been thankful when I've been able to share it with others. In Cleveland one Sunday morning early in the 1964 season, Jerry Kindall of the Indians called me and asked if I'd meet with him for devotions in his room at the Auditorium Hotel.

There were four of us who prayed that morning— Jerry, Don Odle, a coach at Taylor University, Sam Bender, a friend of mine, and I. It was a blessed time and during our hour together Jerry prayed about the fact that he was away from his home in Minneapolis so much. He wanted to be closer, especially at that time, because his wife Georgia was expecting. It had been on his heart for some time and we joined him in asking that God's will would be done.

Not long afterward, Jerry was traded to the Minnesota Twins whose ball park is in Minneapolis. Prayer changes things.

The Yanks clinched the American League pennant early in 1962 but the National League race went right down to the wire with the Giants and Dodgers finishing in a tie. While they battled through playoffs in the Los Angeles Coliseum, our team went down to Candlestick Park in San Francisco, a park we'd never played in. If the Giants won, we'd be familiar with the playing field. As it turned out, we were in the right place.

It was a long Series with the suspense building to the last of the ninth inning in the seventh game. The Yanks were leading by 1 run when Willie Mays doubled with 2 out to put runners on first and third. With Willie Mc-Covey coming to bat, Houk stepped out to the mound to confer with Ralph Terry about walking or pitching to McCovey. Willie had already hit 2 ground balls to me in the Series and I had bobbled both, just barely nipping him at first in each case.

"Don't fumble the ball," Kubek said to me, grinning, "or it will cost us $125,000."

A moment or two later, McCovey hit one of Terry's fast balls for what looked like a base hit and victory for the Giants. But the ball sank and I caught it chest-high, a couple of feet to my left. It was right at me all the way, hard hit, but an easy play.

When the Southern Baptists wrote me that winter, asking if I'd go to Japan in February and give my testimony as part of a nationwide evangelistic campaign, I turned them down. Then a phone call came from Frank Gilliam, a young missionary to Japan, whose heart was burdened and who was traveling all over the United States trying to persuade fellow Baptists, and others too, that the crusade was needed. Frank asked only that I meet him at the Columbia airport and give him thirty minutes to state his case.

I agreed, met him with Johnny Spence, and we went

over to Johnny's house. There Frank explained that the Japanese Baptists were inviting 500 Southern Baptist clergymen to come to Japan and share their faith. Billy Graham was to be the keynote speaker. Don Demeter, then outfielder of the Phillies, and I were being asked to go in advance of the crusade and stimulate public interest.

After we prayed, I agreed to go.

Betsy went with me and we left the children with her mother. In an eight-day period, we covered 26,000 miles, visited missionaries, major league baseball training camps, appeared in church meetings, and were interviewed on Japanese network television.

We were graciously welcomed everywhere and only one newspaper (and that one an American paper) criticized our journey, claiming we were going to Japan "to push the Baptist religion down the throats of the Orientals." It caused Betsy and me to do some real soul-searching. *Was* that our aim? Or were we interested only in sharing the joy of knowing Jesus Christ? We saw how some people could misunderstand and put a denominational tag on the work of the Holy Spirit, and we were determined more than ever to put Christ first, to speak of *Him,* to exalt *Him,* and to please *Him.*

We were thrilled to be able to pay a brief visit to Betsy's aunt, Miss Jenny Alderman, a missionary in nearby Formosa, and to observe her work among the people there.

Then we were on our way back to Fort Lauderdale for the Yankees' spring training. But in our memories we still saw a little old lady bowed down before a temple full of hideous idols. In our ears we could still hear the firecrackers exploding in the back of the temple where the priests went about the business of frightening away evil spirits.

Here was a country where many had never heard the gospel while thousands of Christians meet each night in the great cities of America and the gospel is preached for the benefit of the two or three who may enter and hear it for the first time.

I began to see the tremendous importance of Jesus' command, "Go ye into all the world, and preach the gospel to every creature" (Mark 16:15).

15
Dad Goes Home

THE WINTER OF '62-'63 was the last time I went
hunting with Dad. For several years he hadn't been able
to make the long marches into the bush, so I drove him
back in a jeep, left him off in the middle of a field
where he sat on a small stool. Robby and Ronnie often
came along and stayed with their grandfather to do the
retrieving while I drove to another part of the field to
stir up the doves.

He was always a better shot than I. Five shots and
he'd have four birds.

Once we went duck hunting, my father carrying a
twenty-five-year-old double-barreled 12-gauge shotgun
with hammers. Two birds came in and he nailed one
away out in front, and the other going away. He was
well in his sixties at the time and hadn't shot at a duck
in twelve years.

During the early part of the '63 season there seemed
to be no reason for special concern about Dad's health.
Then, when I was in Baltimore on a road trip, Betsy
called to say that he had had a stroke and had lost his
power of speech.

I flew home and went immediately to the Tuomey Hospital in Sumter. When I entered the room he recognized me but paralysis permitted no expression, no word. I took his hand, spoke to him, then was quiet. A little book of devotions was on the stand beside his bed and I picked it up, reading silently the first piece that met my eye. It was a poem entitled "What Then":

> When the choir has sung its last anthem,
> And the preacher has made his last prayer;
> When the people have heard their last sermon,
> And the sound has died out on the air:
> When the Bible lies closed on the altar,
> And the pews are all empty of men,
> And each one stands facing his record—
> And the great Book is opened—what then?

I knew my father might be dying, and the poem reminded me that some day every one of us must pass that way. It was a sobering thought.

After two days, when Dad's condition had stayed the same, I returned to Baltimore to finish out the Series we were in. Then I flew home again the next Monday.

It was a little less than a month later—after two more visits home—when the phone rang and I knew Dad had died. It was Willie Ann, who had nursed him during his illness. She said that emphysema had cut off his breathing.

During the next few days, which included the funeral and all the arrangements, some relatives were surprised that I showed no outward emotion. Perhaps that was partly because, like so many boys growing up, I'd come to think that tears were a sign of weakness. (I know that in the sad part of a movie I'd often look away from the screen and think of something else to avoid showing my emotion.)

But basically I believe it was because I felt Dad knew the Lord. I sincerely trusted in the Scripture read at the funeral service by Paul Alderman: "But I would not have you to be ignorant, brethren, concerning them which are asleep, that ye sorrow not, even as others which have no hope. For if we believe that Jesus died and rose again, even so them also which sleep in Jesus will God bring with him" (I Thessalonians 4:13-14).

I knew that I would miss him but he'd had a full, active life and was spared more suffering. I knew too that some day there would be a grand reunion.

The press made a big thing of my coming back to work the day after the funeral, but there was no special need for me to stay on in Sumter. My two brothers-in-law, Art Beckstrom and Heyward Strong, and my uncle, George Owens, were a real help to my mother. And I knew Dad would have wanted me to return to the lineup as soon as possible.

We won the pennant again that year and went into the World Series against the Los Angeles Dodgers. Perhaps I should say we went into the Series against Koufax, not to mention Drysdale and a good game pitched by Podres. Anyway, we were beaten 4 straight and there's no point in excuses.

The most lasting memory of that Series was a brief remark made to Betsy by Yogi Berra, when the excitement was over, "How do you think your husband will like playing for me next year?"

A few days later, all the papers carried the big news: Ralph Houk had been promoted to general manager of the Yankee organization and Yogi Berra was the new club manager.

During the winter of '63-'64 I was approached by Billy Zeoli, executive vice president of Gospel Films, Muskegon, Michigan, to be a part of a 45-minute color motion picture, along with Bill Wade (quarterback of the Chicago Bears), Bill Glass, Ray Berry, Alvin Dark (then manager of the San Francisco Giants), and Felipe Alou (Milwaukee Braves' outfielder).

The film "Play for Keeps" was the inspiration of Watson Spoelstra, a Detroit sportswriter, who wanted to find a way to reach the youth of America with the testimonies of Christian athletes.

It was a privilege to be in the film and to appear at premiere showings of it in Hartford, Syracuse, Schenectady, and Poughkeepsie. Each night an average of one thousand young people poured into the prominent downtown theaters where it was presented. During a four-day period, three hundred young people, 90 percent of them boys, made decisions for Christ after the film's showing.

I learned later that a print of "Play for Keeps," with a Japanese soundtrack added, was shown at the Olympic Games in Tokyo.

The glow from this wonderful experience was still on when I reported to Fort Lauderdale in February. We could see from the start that Yogi was really trying in his new job. For years he had been a player and a close friend of many of the other men. Now, seemingly overnight, he had to change roles, take command, make the decisions. In answer to any criticisms of Yogi's managership, I have one answer: he won the pennant.

During a year when nobody on the team was having a really outstanding season, Yogi never stopped believing we were going to make it. Even the famed harmonica incident in August, when we were 6 games out of first place, illustrates the seriousness with which Yogi took the situation.

We'd lost 4 games in a row at Chicago and were on the bus heading back to the airport in bumper-to-bumper traffic. Nobody was talking. In the back of the bus, Phil Linz, our utility infielder, trotted out a newly purchased harmonica and blew an exploratory toot-toot on it. Up front, Yogi turned around, frowning, but didn't speak.

Absorbed in his new instrument, Phil gave another toot-toot. This time Yogi turned around and in so many words asked him to put away the harmonica. But over the traffic noise Phil only half-heard the remark.

"What'd he say?" he inquired of several players who were beginning to take notice.

"He said, go ahead and play some more. He likes it."

With that encouragement, Phil put the instrument to his mouth and toot-toot-tooted again. Yogi bounded up and started for the rear of the bus, blood in his eye. Too late Phil saw he'd been given incorrect information about the boss's wishes and, as Yogi bore down on him, he tossed the harmonica to him. Yogi caught it and in the same angry motion flipped it away. It bounced off Joe Pepitone's chin and from there into every sports page in the country.

Some writers think that was the turning point. I don't. We went on to Boston where we lost still another game. *Then* we started to climb—and the reasons were hustle, alertness, good pitching and hitting.

Our September drive seemed almost to be the trademark of the team that had won 26 American League pennants and 20 World Championships since 1921. And unbelievably the Orioles and White Sox faltered as we continued to drive all the way to the pennant.

Providing great help along the way were young Mel Stottlemeyre and Ralph Houk's first major trade, Pete Ramos, who contributed outstanding pitching.

We won, a day before the end of the season, and Yogi carried his victorious team back to his old hometown, St. Louis. It was an exciting Series, with every game close. The difference in the games resulted from an error here, a homerun there.

When I made the last out, I was painfully aware that if I'd been able to get a base hit, the big sluggers on our club might have been able to pull a Series victory out of the fire.

I was also conscious of the fact that in two of the games, I'd made errors that opened the door to defeat for our team.

16
What About Errors?

IT'S WONDERFUL TO hit a game-winning homerun and give the glory to God. And everybody is impressed by a football, basketball, or baseball player who is humble in the midst of acclaim. But who *wouldn't* be willing to have a try at humility at the *top* of the ladder?

At one time my idea of a completely happy life was an uninterrupted series of personal successes—with God glorified in each one.

But what about failure and defeat?

I'd gone to the All-Star game in July of '63 and lost the game for the American League almost single-handedly. I was 0-for-5 at the plate and I committed a damaging error in the field.

My two errors in the '64 Series may well have been the difference between winning and losing for the Yankees. There's no excuse for these errors and no way to erase them from the record books.

I didn't feel like talking after the '64 Series. Over and over I relived the plays I'd bobbled, tasting bitter, helpless regret. But I was missing the point.

Gradually the Lord's peace and love began to penetrate my disappointment as Betsy reminded me of Romans 8:28: ". . . we know that all things work together for good to them that love God, to them who are the called according to his purpose."

All things? Even errors, hitting into double plays, striking out? How can God get any glory from those things?

My mind went back to the afternoon when I was fourteen and the pastor came to call at our house. I was a kid like a thousand other kids, just interested in baseball. It must have been raining that day—I can't remember—because, if it hadn't, I would have been outside, playing.

But God had mercy on me. I was home that day and I sat still enough for a half hour to hear a man tell me that the Son of God loved me enough to die for me.

That day I accepted Jesus Christ as my personal Saviour, and each succeeding year has shown me how important my decision was. It's a wonderful thing to know your sins are forgiven.

Just one illustration: In a game at Los Angeles, I was facing Eli Grba of the Angels, a former Yankee teammate. Anger flared in me when a close pitch knicked my uniform.

"I ought to punch you right in the nose!" I told him as I went down to first on a walk.

"You and who else?" Eli retorted.

He gave way to a relief pitcher by the time I got over

to third base and as he walked off the field he said, "Ritchie, I wasn't throwing at you. The ball just slipped."

It's great to know that Eli didn't hold my angry blowup against me. But it's even greater to know that God, because of Jesus Christ, has forgiven me.

Year after year I've been impressed with the great salvation that became mine at fourteen. And more than this, I've come to see that Jesus is my *Lord.* I'm His personal property and everything I do is His business.

This, then, was the answer to my question after the '64 Series. This is how all things—homeruns and costly errors—"work together for good" in my life. It's because He's in charge. It's because I love Him and want to please Him in every possible way.

And that's why He doesn't need my successes to glorify His name. He can do it, perhaps even better, when I fail.

"For by grace are ye saved through faith; and that not of yourselves: it is the gift of God: Not of works, lest any man should boast. For we are his workmanship, created in Christ Jesus unto good works, which God hath before ordained that we should walk in them" (Ephesians 2:8-10).

GOD'S HALL OF FAME

The ultimate in a baseball player's career is to achieve recognition in the Hall of Fame. The following poem, "God's Hall of Fame," by Walt Huntley, expresses my outlook on baseball and life.

Your name may not appear down here
In this world's Hall of Fame,
In fact, you may be so unknown
That no one knows your name;
The oscars and the praise of men
May never come your way,
But don't forget God has rewards
That He'll hand out someday.

This Hall of Fame is only good
As long as time shall be;
But keep in mind, God's Hall of Fame
Is for eternity;
To have your name inscribed up there
Is greater more by far
Than all the fame and all the praise
Of ev'ry man-made star.

This crowd on earth they soon forget
    When you're not at the top,
They'll cheer like mad until you fall
    And then their praise will stop;
Not God, He never does forget,
    And in His Hall of Fame,
By just believing on His Son,
    Forever—there's your name.

I tell you, friend, I wouldn't trade
    My name, however small,
That's written there beyond the stars
    In that celestial Hall,
For all the famous names on earth,
    Or glory that they share;
I'd rather be an unknown here,
    And have my name up there.

WALT HUNTLEY
(Used by permission)